Learning How to Heal Heart

Learning How to Heal a Broken Heart

Transforming Breakdowns into Breakthroughs

Marvin Scholz

Dedication:

To Larry:

Thank you for supporting me, for believing in me, and for making such a positive impact in my life. You've nurtured my passion while being there for me when my dreams were crushed. The respect I have for you is endless. I am truly honored to have you in my life. You are one of the greatest men I know. I pray that one day I'll be as good a man as you are. You deserve only the best things in this world. Fortunately for you, you already have all you need. A man on his own can accomplish many things. But a great man with a great woman by his side; the possibilities will be endless. Patricia, you have a heart of gold. You two give me hope. I love the love you two share. Never give up on each other.

To Sandra:

Thank you for walking this journey with me. It's been a long road, but we made it. We survived. It's time to be happy again. For both of us.

To Christian:

Where do I even begin? This book wouldn't have been written if it wasn't for you. You are my dearest friend. I cherish you like no other. You were there for me at a point in my life when I didn't think I could go on. I was so close to giving up, but you reminded me that happiness can be found in even the darkest of times. Thank you for comforting me when I was too broken to comfort myself. You were my lighthouse, my compass that led me out of my brokenness. When I was drowning in immeasurable grief, you taught me how to swim. I can't thank you enough. You saved me. 145 words aren't enough to express my gratitude. But I suppose it's a start. Please follow your dreams, you have no idea of the potential for greatness that lies within you.

Table of Contents

x

Introduction:

I could give you a hundred reasons as to why I wrote this book, and I could give you a thousand reasons as to why you should read this book. I could tell you that my situation was unique, unprecedented even. But truth be told, it wasn't. We all go through stuff in life. At one point or another, we will all end up on this road. Some more often than others. But sometimes, we all end up breaking. Sometimes we don't just break, but instead, we shatter into a million pieces. Our dreams shatter, our hopes and our plans for the future fall apart. Suddenly, we are left with nothing but dust. And when that happens, we need to heal. The right way. Deep and genuine healing is required when we break.

In all my years on this planet, I have yet to meet someone who has not been heartbroken at least once in their life. It happens to us all, more often than not, it'll happen more than once. We get heartbroken, we get disappointed, we get rejected. It's part of life. We live in a world with flawed humans who fail us and make mistakes. Many of our dreams are wrapped up in these humans, and because of that, brokenness is just a part of living on this earth.

It's a price of admission to this life and something which we all must pay. We can't always control the situation or the outcome for that matter. But we can control how we respond to the devastating blow when heartbreak strikes. In this book, I will go over all the ways one can truly heal from heartbreak. Dealing with the pain that comes with it, the struggle, the insecurities, disappointment, and the rejection. I will show you how to combat grief and how to endure the difficult road to becoming whole again.

Heartbreak and disappointment, they change you; change how you eat, how you sleep, and how you interact with others. It shakes you to your very core. The essence of who you are. Recovering from such trauma can be an extremely lengthy and challenging process. If done incorrectly, you're not only prolonging your heartbreak but also risking long-term emotional damage.

Add to the fact that most people don't even know what genuine healing really is, and then you understand why most people never truly accomplish it.

In a world that leaves us broken many times over, we must excel in the process of healing. Healing is an art. An art that we must master if we want to live a truly fulfilling life. If we're going to create healthy, long-lasting relationships, then we have to learn how to heal fully, and in the right away from the ones that leave us broken. Because heartbreak isn't physical trauma where our bodies automatically know how to respond. No, I'm afraid with mental trauma, the healing process is far more complicated than that. And it's entirely up to us whether we heal or not.

I mentioned that the situation that led me to write this book wasn't unique. And it wasn't. I'm not the first person who had to deal with heartbreak. I'm not the first person who's been rejected, lied to, or disappointed. None of these unfortunate events happened for the first time. But in my not-so-unique situation, I found a unique way to rationalize the pain that I incurred, and how to use that pain as a catalyst for change. I found a way to let the breaking, be my making.

It wasn't easy, it wasn't painless, and it wasn't pretty, but I sure made it out of the heartbreak alive. Better than ever. Now it's my turn to help you find your way back home again. I'm here to help you turn your breaking into your making.

I am here to teach you how you can turn your heartbreak into artwork. I am here to show you how to climb out of the abyss that you're currently trapped in. I know it must feel like you're drowning in immense disappointment, but I'm here now, I'll pull you out of this mess. I'll teach you how to endure this heart-wrenching process.

If your heart is heavy, if your soul is crushed, if you're suffocating immeasurable grief and disappointment, I want you to take this book and let it be your lifeline for these troublesome times. Let me be the compass that will lead you out of this storm.

I'm here to guide you on this journey, the journey towards healing. Be your voice of reason, your shoulder to cry on. I'm your biggest supporter. I'm rooting for you. Because I've been where you've been. I know the feeling. The feeling like you've lost everything. Lost yourself. I know it'll get better, but you don't. That is why I'm here. I promise I'll stay by your side until the end. Unlike others, I will not abandon you. Step by step, day by day, you'll be whole again. Follow my lead. We'll get through this together.

Let's go!

Part 1: [Face The Music]

1.1 Admitting You Are Hurt

I recently started something that I've wanted to do for a very long time; Muay Thai training. For the people who don't know what that is, let me explain. Muay Thai is a combat sport that originated in Thailand. It involves stand-up striking and various clinching techniques to render your opponent into submission. In Muay Thai, you are allowed to use your fists, elbows, knees, and shins, making it a mighty and strenuous combat sport.

In one of my very first sessions, I quickly learned just how demanding this sport really is. I was sparring with another Muay Thai enthusiast. It just so happened that this fellow Muay Thai "enthusiast" turned out to be a professional kickboxer out of Spain. This was a fact that everyone in that gym had failed to mention, by the way. Anyways; so there I am sparring with this professional fighter, not knowing that I am about to get rocked. For those of you who don't know what "sparring" is, it's a form of training that mimics the particular combat sport. It's essentially fighting at half speed or so – same techniques and movements, just with a little less force. As it turned out, his half-speed wasn't my half speed.

Not even a minute into the round, and I ended up getting hit with a sturdy left hook. I was left astonished, and not in a good way. I can still feel that punch today. It hurt like hell, and not necessarily because of its strength, although I'm sure that had something to do with it. But more importantly, the reason why I was so surprised by the attack was that I didn't expect it. I didn't see it coming. Filled with rage and embarrassment, I scrambled around in the ring, trying to land blows at my opponent that were equally powerful to get payback. I spent so much energy trying to force a strike, that I tired myself out and got into even more trouble. I ended up losing miserably. Yet there was a lesson to be found in this sad beatdown.

My trainer brought up a simple yet profound point. He said: "Son, you're going to get hit, there's no question about it. The only question is, how will you respond to the hit"?

I'm not sure which was louder; my trainer yelling at me, or the ringing noise my ear was making from that vicious hit?

Pay attention! I am going to give you a huge piece of advice. One that doesn't come with having to get punched in the face. I took that burden on for you. You're welcome. You may not have gotten hit in the face, but you're heartbroken, and that hurts a thousand times more than a punch to the face from a professional kickboxer. You need to expect it to hurt. You need to prepare for the hit, for the pain, and for the agony that will follow. As hard as this might be to hear right now, it's perfectly normal to feel like this. In fact, its an essential part of the healing process and something you need to go through.

I am not going to sugarcoat things; the next few weeks and months will, without a doubt, suck. It's going to hurt, and it's going to hurt a lot. Acknowledging it is the first step that you will need to take to begin this long, mournful journey of healing.

Acknowledging what's about to happen and accepting that things will be difficult for quite some time is crucial if you want to heal yourself in the right way.

Don't act shocked when it hurts, don't be taken by surprise when you feel like the ground is being stripped from under you. Don't be like me in that ring, running around like a madman wondering why in the heck I got hit. I got hit because I'm fighting someone in a ring, simple. You loved and got hurt, it happens. It's part of the package called 'life.' We all go through it. Don't deny it, accept it. Admit that you're hurting and face any challenges that lie ahead head-on.

Stop asking why heartbreak hurts so much. Know that it's supposed to feel this way. You're human. You're going to hurt. You are going to want to cry and breakdown. This is normal, and it's not something to be ashamed of. Face the music; heartbreak sucks no matter what, and no matter whether you caused it or not.

1.2 Brace for Impact

No one wakes up in the morning and says:" well, gee, it's a beautiful day to get heartbroken." No one plans to get disappointed, to get let down, to get betrayed. It happens unexpectedly and often without remorse. It hits us like a devastating earthquake. But fighting this heartbreak is about knowing that it's about to get a heck of a lot worse. It's imperative to understand that the journey towards healing is a long and dark one, that isn't easily accomplished.

Heartbreak is hard, healing correctly from it is a lot harder. Understanding that and preparing for that simple fact of reality is just as important as any other healing part. Brace yourself for the storm that is about to disrupt your life. The vicious ups and downs, the mixed emotions, the sleepless nights, the dreary mornings, the perplexing weeks, and months that are yet to come. It's time to brace for impact. A storm is coming, one that you cannot outrun or outmaneuver. There's no shelter, and no escaping it. It's coming, and there is nothing that you can do except face it. Knowing what you're about to walk into is critical if you want to heal.

All you can do, all anyone can do is to walk through it. Push through it. You can't ride it out somewhere safe, you have to ride through it. Prepare yourself mentally and physically that it will get worse before it gets better. Before you embark on this journey towards deep and genuine healing, know that it goes down before it goes up. That's just the way it is. There's no skipping this process. No pretending that it will be okay in this very instant. It will be okay, but just not now. Not tomorrow, not for a very long time. But you will get through this storm, we will get through this together.

1.3 It's Okay to Not Be Okay

You know how people ask you how you're doing after a breakup, and you'll easily brush them off? "I'm fine." Or "I'm okay." News flash; you're not okay. I don't care what you're trying to tell yourself. "I didn't care about him." "I'm already over her." "He was nothing to me." You can tell yourself whatever you want, but I know the truth. You're not fine. And you won't be for a very long time. You don't have to pretend like everything is okay. Like everything is all good. Because it isn't. It couldn't possibly be okay. Your 4-year relationship just ended two weeks ago, and you're 'okay,' really? How exactly does that work? As a society, we are so focused on hiding our pain and pretending like everything is fine, that we are willing to lie to the people who love us, just to come across as tough or strong. We know we aren't okay. You know you're dying inside, so why lie? Why not admit the defeat, the loss, the heartache? Why pretend? Because you want to be viewed as unphased and secure, right?

If you were to break your arm playing sports, would you still tell people that you're okay? If you were to get into a severe car accident that left you lying in the hospital for 2 days, would you still tell people that you're doing okay? I don't think so.

Just because heartbreak isn't physical damage, it doesn't mean it hurts any less. In fact, a broken heart is often more severe than a broken bone.

So let's stop with the charade. Let's stop pretending that heartbreak isn't a big deal. Because the truth of the matter is that, yes, it is a big deal. It's a huge deal. Heartbreak comes with many challenges that we must face, and simply 'getting over it' doesn't cut it. And neither does pretending that everything is fine.

So the next time someone asks you how you are doing, know that it is okay to not be okay. You don't have to be ashamed of your mourning, of your heartache, of your disappointment. If you want to heal from the physiological injuries that heartbreak causes (which I'm assuming you do since you're reading this book), then you'll need to accept the simple truth that right now, you're not okay, and you won't be for some time. And that's just the reality of things.

Admitting to that truth is crucial if we want to heal.

1.4 What is Healing, And Why Do We Need It?

Admitting that we are hurt and understanding that it's okay to not be okay is only the beginning of our long road to healing. For us to genuinely heal, we first must understand what healing really is, and why we all need it after a heartbreaking loss or painful disappointment.

Throughout our time on this earth, we will all sustain dozens, if not hundreds of physical injuries. Some will be the size of paper cuts, others will cover entire areas of our bodies. But with all physical injuries, our body is a master at healing itself. We don't even have to tell it what to do. It simply knows how to respond to physical trauma.

When I was in high school, I used to play football. I wasn't the best, but I definitely wasn't the worst. One day at the end of my junior year, I somehow ended up finding the only hole in the ground on our practice field and stepped right into it. Like I said; I wasn't the best.

This little accident resulted in me breaking my ankle. This was over 9 years ago, and I can still remember the pain like it was yesterday.

My ankle instantly became the size of a baseball. The pain was excruciating. I could barely get up. At first, our athletic trainer at the time thought it was just a severe sprain. Only a week later, however, did I find out that I actually managed to break part of the bone.

Invisible to the naked eye, but clearly noticeable with the help of an X-Ray, did the doctor figure out what was wrong.

See, my body suffered severe physical trauma, and the way it protected itself was by creating the swelling to immobilize me. To keep me off my feet. My body created the pain to signal me that there was something wrong, to stop me from doing what I was doing and deal with whatever was wrong.

The pain kept me out of the game, and the swelling protected the tissue from further damage. Your body is designed to protect itself. It's made to endure and to persevere. This is what our body does when we get physically injured. Heartbreak, on the other hand, will trigger physiological injuries that our body is not so well equipped to fight. The undoubted truth is that we do not know how to deal with heartbreak. As smart as we humans may be, we are awfully clueless when it comes to our own mental wellbeing. We don't have to tell our bodies how to heal a broken bone, but we do have to tell our minds how to overcome the loss of a loved one.

When I stepped into that hole and broke my ankle, if there was no pain, if there were no swelling, I would have kept on playing the game. Maybe I would have made it through the drive or even the game, but sooner or later, it would have caught up with me. If I had ignored the pain and kept playing through it, I would have inevitably hurt myself even more.

I ended up being out for the rest of the season and for most of the summer. I had to wear a cast for almost two months to protect the bone and let my body do its healing.

Healing is the process of overcoming a trauma that we've sustained. The length of healing that is required depends on the severity of the trauma and the individual involved.

Everyone is different, and every injury is unique, but everyone needs to heal properly to prevent further damage. If we don't heal right, if we skip the entire process, we risk carrying all this hurt and grief with us into the next relationship. And the next one, and the one after that. We'll risk carrying all that pain with us, and we'll end up bleeding on people who didn't even cause the injury to begin with. Why? All because we didn't take the time and energy to heal properly in the first place.

If we truly want to heal from heartbreak, then we need to understand this. Because we cannot fix what we don't understand. How can you grow from something if you don't even see the reason for the growth? How can you overcome something that you do not see coming?

1.5 Pain Has A Purpose

There is a reason why you are currently feeling what you're feeling. There's a reason for the pain. Pain signals to the body that there is something wrong. Something that requires your full and undivided attention. You don't suffer from pain for no reason.

When you sustain a physical injury, your body will send signals to your brain that there is something wrong. Something requires fixing. And when that happens, you don't just ignore the pain, do you? You don't just pretend your ankle isn't sprained. You don't just pretend that you're not sick.

No, instead, you assess the situation, maybe go see a doctor and find a diagnosis to your injury or illness and start looking for a treatment plan or solution. You fix the issue. You try and heal any sickness or damage that you've sustained.

Just like physical pain has a purpose; the purpose of protecting you or preventing further damage; heartbreak, and emotional pain also has a purpose. What you need to do when that heartbreak is occurring is to stop and assess the situation. Analyze the damage, see what went wrong and where, and then acquire a treatment plan. Don't try to pretend like the pain isn't there. Don't skip the healing process.

You need to feel everything you need to feel. Get rid of the distractions. Stop trying to numb the pain. Stop trying to skip the steps that your body and mind need to heal and overcome the trauma it has sustained.

Because heartbreak and disappointment are both severe traumas to your body. You may not physically be able to see them, but trust me, they are real, and they are there. They are deep inside of you, invisible to the naked eye. But they're wreaking havoc inside of you. Like cancer. Turning your world upside down. And if you don't

12

treat the heartbreak right then and there, it'll spread throughout your entire body.

Deep healing requires a deep understanding of what is going on. An acknowledgment of the pain. It's accepting what needs to be accepted, that we've suffered a tremendous loss in our life. That, for better or worse, nothing will ever be the same. It's about embracing the pain. It's about rebuilding yourself up after the storm has passed and devastated your very existence. Deep healing is acknowledging that you may not have caused this trauma, but it's your responsibility to heal from it. You owe it to yourself.

Part 2: [No Room For Pride]

2.1 Forgiveness

To truly heal and move on from our traumatic experience, we all must do one thing, something that many of us struggle with. We must learn how to forgive before we can truly let go and in turn, move on. We must forgive past mistakes, the regrets, the wrong choices.

In my life, I've made many mistakes. Looking back, my past is tainted, filled with darkness and regret. I'm not proud of many things that I've done. The people I've hurt. I'm sorry to everyone who has been affected by my poor choices, and my poor, and often lacking judgment. I'm sorry for wronging you.

Ironically enough, though, I've also been hurt in ways that I don't even want to begin to describe. I couldn't tell you which is worse; hurting someone you love or being hurt by the one person who you believed would never hurt you. I've been on both ends of the spectrum. And to be honest, neither of them are good places to be. But the truth of the matter is that at one point or another, we will all end up on either side. Chances are, we'll be on both at some point.

We, humans, are, by nature, flawed. We make mistakes. We hurt people we love. We exercise poor judgment. I'm not trying to make excuses for our behavior. Hurting someone you love is never okay, nor is it acceptable. But it happens. You need to understand that. Forgiving yourself for hurting a person you love is hard, incredibly hard. Trust me, I know. I've been there. The guilt that keeps you up at night that won't let you go. The shame that is robbing you of your peace. You feel unworthy of forgiveness, even worse, people will often make you feel like you don't deserve forgiveness because of your mistakes.

But you must forgive yourself if you genuinely want to heal. You're not perfect, and you never will be. No one is, and no one ever will be. Your mistakes do not define you. Nor do they give anyone the right to tell you what you are and what you are not worthy of. So stop letting your past prevent you from forgiving yourself. We all have done things that we aren't proud of, but that shouldn't stop us from forgiving ourselves.

Forgiving yourself is hard, but perhaps even harder is forgiving a person who isn't even sorry for wronging you, who doesn't even realize the damage that they've done. They're not sorry. They're not trying to fix their mistake; they're not trying to reconcile. They simply do not care.

Yet we still have to forgive them. If we're going to move on, then we have to so that we can truly let them go.

Forgiveness means giving up hope for a different past. It's accepting that the past is just that, the past. It's over. What's done is done. Forgiveness is about coming to terms with the fact that the dust has settled, and the destruction left in its wake can never be reconstructed to resemble what it was. There is no going back, no makeovers, no second chances.

Forgiveness is accepting that yes, maybe you caused the hurricane, or perhaps you didn't, but the devastation has taken place, and even though it may be unfair, you still have to live in its devastation.

Forgiveness means accepting responsibility – not necessarily for causing the destruction, but for cleaning it up. It's the decision that restoring your own peace is finally a bigger priority than hoping for that person to come running back into your arms.

It's about realizing that only you can put yourself back together. Forgiveness is accepting that they wounded you so profoundly, the scars may remain for a lifetime. But as we'll discuss later on, scars can be beautiful too.

So forgive yourself for all the mistakes you've made. It may be a breakup, but you know what else I'd call it? A clean slate. The chance to start afresh. Forgive yourself for the lies, the distrust, the jealousy, and for all the pain you've caused. Forgive yourself utterly and wholeheartedly. You deserve this as much as anyone. Don't let anyone tell you otherwise. Don't let someone tell you that you're not worthy of forgiveness. Because guess what? You are worth it.

But if we forgive ourselves for our mistakes, we also must forgive the people who've wronged us. The ones who broke us damaged us, lied, betrayed, and tarnished us. The ones that lead us on, and manipulated us into believing we aren't worth it. The ones who walked away, the ones who abandoned us. We must forgive them, even if they never asked for our forgiveness. Even if they're not sorry, even if they don't have an ounce of remorse. We must let them off the hook as well if we genuinely want to continue this journey to deep healing.

On your path to healing, you'll realize that you have to find peace with never receiving an apology from people who are unable to recognize their faults. That's just who they are, and you have to accept that.

Forgiveness doesn't mean you're going to be best friends with the person who hurt you either, it doesn't mean you have to endorse what they've done to you. Forgiveness is not forgetting what has happened. It just means accepting that they've left a mark on you. A mark that is now your burden to bear. It means you're done waiting for the person who broke you to come put you back together.

Forgiveness means to let bygones be bygones. Forgiveness is letting go. And we must let go if we want to heal.

2.2 Owning Your Mistake

I'm a big believer in accountability. I believe that the road to deep and genuine healing is one that begins with owning up to your mistakes and flaws. If we want to forgive ourselves, we must first acknowledge the pain that we've caused. I don't know what you've done, I don't know who you've hurt. But what I do know is that you need to own your mistakes. You don't have to be proud of them to own them. Owning your mistakes is accepting that you've wronged someone. That you had a lapse in judgment. Maybe even a dozen lapses. What matters is that at this very moment, your mistakes do not matter, the only thing that matters moving forward is what you'll be able to learn from them.

We all mess up. We all screw up. It happens.

The only question is how you will respond to your mistake. Will you let it define you? Will you act like it doesn't matter? Will you continue to behave the same way?

Owning your mistake means being remorseful. Being remorseful doesn't mean saying: "I'm sorry I've hurt you, I didn't mean to." No, that isn't owning up to your mistake, and it isn't remorseful.

You are genuinely remorseful when you say, "I made a mistake, I don't want to make the same or similar mistake again, what can I do to ensure that something like this will never happen again?"

Being remorseful and owning up to your mistake isn't about saying sorry, it's about ensuring that you'll never have to say sorry again for the same reason.

You're going to make mistakes in this life, there's no question about it. But the goal is to not repeat the same or similar mistake over and over again and continue to hurt people.

It isn't right. So own up to your mistake, analyze the situation, and learn from it. That's what life is all about. That's what healing is all about. It's a learning experience.

But if we genuinely want to heal, we need to own up to our mistakes. Owning up to them isn't necessarily the same as holding on to them, but learning from your mistakes is crucial if we genuinely want to be whole again.

2.3 Ask "How" Not "Why"

We, humans, are obsessed with asking "why." It starts off as young children. Have you ever noticed how kids ask a hundred questions? And they all start off with "why." Why is the sky blue? Why do I need 8 hours of sleep and not 2? Why do I have to eat all my veggies? Why do I have to brush my teeth before bed?

If you're a parent, then you know this is true. If you have little siblings, nephews, or nieces, you'll know this as well. Children want to understand why things are happening. And as we get older, we realize that this lust for answers never truly goes away. No matter if we're 6 or 26.

When we suffered a life-altering loss, we automatically want to know why it happened. Why did they leave? Why did they lie to me? Why did he choose her and not me? Why am I not good enough? Why is this happening to me?

The list goes on and on. The quest for answers never stops when we're heartbroken. And if you're not careful, that quest will consume you. The worst part about this is that none of those questions will help you heal any faster, if anything, they'll only prolong your healing process. Because no response will ever quench that thirst you have for answers. No answer will ever be sufficient. They left because they wanted to. They lied because they wanted to. They disappointed you because they chose to.

But wanting to know why things went wrong, won't bring you any closer to finding closure. Instead of asking "why," try asking "how." Replace the thought: "why did she leave me?" with "how can I learn from this experience?". See what we're doing here? We no longer ask why the bad things had to happen. Instead, we focus on learning from those bad things.

What's done is done. Why bother asking why when you could spend your time asking how you'll become better from this loss.

Finding out why someone hurt you doesn't undo the damage they caused, but asking how you can learn from this experience will help stimulate growth. It'll be a massive step towards profound healing.

Let go of the why mentality and adopt the how attitude instead. Stop being a victim to your unfortunate circumstances, and instead be a victor.

So the next time you find your mind wandering to all the "why's," stop, count to three, and redirect your thoughts to how questions instead. Do this every day, and with each day, it'll get easier. At first, you'll have to force yourself to change your thinking. But after a while, it'll become natural. It'll be how you heal.

2.4 Get Comfortable With Being Uncomfortable

The path to deep healing is a long one that is filled with darkness and agony. I won't lie to you; this journey will be hard. It may be the hardest thing you'll ever have to do. But you can do this. We can do this. I'm right here by your side.

You have to understand that on this journey, you're going to be uncomfortable for a while. This is just a reality of things. It won't be easy, it won't be fun, and it won't be quick. You heal by becoming profoundly uncomfortable. You embrace the pain, the sorrow, and the loss.

You visit all the places you and your partner have been and reclaim them. The place he took you for your first date. The movie-theater were you two first kissed. The ice cream place by your house that you religiously visited together. The Italian restaurant where you were regulars because that was 'your spot.' The routine you both had. The pizza dates, the Netflix dates, the breakfast dates. All of it, you do again. But this time, it's just you.

You visit these places. Places that you thought you'd never have to go alone. And this time, you hold your own hand as you go. You're going to cry and miss them. You're going to be miserable, but you're going to do it because you need to get uncomfortable if you ever want to be comfortable again without them by your side. You need to become uncomfortable if you're going to heal right.

Don't lie to yourself about how this is going to be easy and effortless - not yet. First, you dive right into the deepest part of missing them. It's a deep ocean of pain and misery. But you will jump in it. You will let the pain consume you. You will feel their absence deep inside your core. You absorb it in exactly the way that you're afraid of it. You let it sink under your skin. Let it take over every single fiber of your body. Every breath, every thought, and every idea will entail them.

If this sounds painful to you, it's because it is. But this is precisely what you need to do. You need to feel everything that you're feeling, and you need to embrace it. Don't try to outrun the pain, because you can't heal by avoiding this situation that you've been placed in.

I had to get incredibly uncomfortable on my journey towards healing. There was a woman I loved. She was my life, my heart. She was enormously important to me. I remember the first date that she and I were on. I remember it like it was yesterday. We ended up on the beach at night in one of those lifeguard towers. With a bottle of wine and endless hours to talk. I can still hear the waves crashing onto the shore. I can still remember her crashing into my life. That night, I will never forget.

To truly part ways with this person, to truly let her go, I knew I would have to get uncomfortable. So I went back to the place where we had our first date and sat out on the very same lifeguard tower where over 2 years ago, we had sat together. I looked out into the ocean, seeing the waves crash onto the beach and felt everything I needed to feel. I felt her absence, I felt her loss. I felt the pain, and I felt the agony. For hours I sat there. It wasn't that I enjoyed it, but I knew I needed it. I knew that for me to become whole again, I had to let the pain consume me first.

I had to cleanse my body of those emotions. And that cleanse starts with accepting that you're going to be insanely uncomfortable. Feeling the pain is one of the first steps toward healing emotional trauma. The longer we avoid the feeling, the longer we delay the healing.

So get ready to be uncomfortable for a very long time. This won't be pretty, but once all is said and done, things will be pretty remarkable for you.

2.5 Promise Me You'll Grieve

I promised you at the beginning of this book that I would stay with you until the end. And I intend to honor that promise. I'm here for you, and I'll walk with you through this storm. But I want you to promise me something in return.

Promise me that you'll grieve. Don't run away from your problems. Face them. I'm sure it feels like you're staring into an abyss right now, but until you mourn, you won't be able to cross it.

Feel everything that you need to feel. Cry, scream, yell, whatever it is that you're feeling inside of you right now, let it out.

We associate the word grief with death, but that's precisely what the end of a relationship is. It's the death of all the dreams you two shared. Death to a million promises. Death to hope for the future with that someone. The end of a relationship is the end of a world that you had planned and that you had envisioned.

So, therefore, I urge you to treat heartbreak in such a manner. The person that you loved has left, they're gone. And they won't ever return. Realizing that, and understanding it takes time, it takes courage, and it takes grief. So please promise me that you will grieve their loss. Mourn their absence.

This doesn't happen in a day, or a week, or even a month for that matter. It takes time, my God does it take time. Don't skip this stage because you will not be able to heal if you don't grieve properly.

I became awfully familiar with what grieving the loss of someone who is still alive, is like. I mourned the fact that I would never see her smile again. I'd never hear her voice again. Never get to kiss her again. Never board another plane with her. I had to come to terms with the fact that I will never make another memory with her again. I had to mourn and grieve. And it has taken me months to complete this process. But it's something that needs to be done if we ever want to find our way to healing.

2.6 It's Time to Turn Around

In order for us to heal, we must look at what lies ahead instead of what is behind us. You can't go into what's next that has your name on it by looking backward. Your next assignment, your next blessing, your next breakthrough, your next season. You can't receive without first releasing. What happened, happened. It happened. Whether you wanted it to or not. Whether it was your fault or not. It happened. Acknowledge it. You were disappointed. Stuff happened to you that broke your heart. I get it. But you can't experience the purpose that God has for you, with your head in the past. You simply cannot. It's time to turn around.

You can't continue on this journey towards healing by facing your past, and you can't continue by facing other people. You cannot look at them and compare yourself to them and compare your situation to theirs. You're not them, and they're not you. Your destiny is different than theirs. God has something else planned for you. Stop looking at other people for answers. Everything you need is right within you. They cannot help you, not in going into the future that God has planned just for you. It's turnaround time, and only you can do this. It's time to look ahead. Time to look upwards. Above the dust, away from the past and away from distractions. It's time to turn around. Time to turn your life around. Time to get back on that horse and live your life to the fullest. Life's too short to be heartbroken for too long. Make peace with what's behind you, and put your eyes on the joy that's ahead of you.

Part 3 [Release]

3.1 Let Go

It's time, you hear me. We've reached the hardest part of this book. The part that will take the longest, the part that will be the hardest. The part that will cause the most heartache. It is time to let go. We've reached a crossroads on this long dreadful journey towards healing.

This part will dictate how we continue moving forward. I told you we'd walk this journey together. But we cannot continue towards deep healing until we cross this part. And I cannot do this for you. You have to take that step. You need to let go.

I know letting go feels like the hardest thing in the world to do right now, but it'll get easier when you learn how to love yourself. When you finally put yourself first.

I know you don't want to let go because you've invested so much time and energy into this person and that giving up seems like an awfully foolish mistake. All the years of building a life with someone, just to walk away. All the memories, the dreams, the hopes. All gone. It's something you deeply struggle with. I know, because I too have been there. I feel your pain.

You want to hold on, you want to cling to your past with the hopes that somehow things could just maybe go back to how they used to be. That they come back. That there is a way to reconcile. But the sad truth is, there isn't. They aren't coming back because they do not care. You need to understand that. So it's time to put yourself first. To put your own happiness above the desire to be with someone who doesn't want to be with you. The person you once knew, no longer exists. They're a sheer memory of your past. A ghost. So stop letting them haunt you. It's time to let go.

Let go of the memories, the dreams, the hopes, and the wishful thinking.

3.2 - Stop Waiting, Stop Hoping

The longer you wait for them to come back, the longer you will prolong your healing. It doesn't matter if you were the one who caused this disastrous breakup, the only thing that matters is that it happened. They are gone, and they won't come back, so stop waiting for a day that'll never come.

This has been by far the hardest lesson I've had to learn on this journey. Don't make the same mistake that I made.

I waited 6 months for someone to come back who never intended to return in the first place. I waited for half a year. Maybe not directly, but the hope was always there. That person led me to believe that there was a way to reconcile. She made me think that she just needed 'more time.' I made a mistake that ended the relationship, and so I thought I had to stick around and be available to her whenever she was ready to talk to me.

She saw me becoming a better person. Saw the changes, saw the growth. She didn't want me, but she couldn't see me happy with someone else. She came into my life when she wanted, and she left when she wanted. I loved that woman more than anything in this world, so of course, every minute she reached out, I jumped at the opportunity to reconcile. To fix my mistake. But see, she never forgave me, and she never intended on working things out. Instead, she manipulated me into believing I wasn't good enough for her. Questioning my motives, asking me who I was talking to.

Interrogating me, doubting me. All to just then leave again. For 6 months, this game continued. Back and forth. I didn't reach out to her, I tried making peace with her decision. I accepted it. But she would find any way to reach out to me. And I was foolish enough to give in because, well, I loved her. She destroyed me in her quest for closure.

What I put her through, she didn't deserve. Not remotely. But what she put me through for 6 months, constitutes to be nothing short of mental abuse. She destroyed me, broke me down. And then left me to pick up the broken pieces by myself when she finally had enough. She used me. Weaned herself off of me while I confused it for a sign of hope. She chose her own closure at the expense of my peace.

I made many mistakes in my life, and in that relationship. But until this day, my biggest mistake was holding on to the idea that there was hope for the two of us.

I am sharing this with you because I need you to understand that if someone cannot forgive you for your mistakes, then you need to let them go. 'More time' is not going to be the answer here. If they say they need more time, run the other way. As fast as you can. Either you work through things together, or you part ways. If you're reading this, I suppose you're in need of the latter.

I can't stress enough how imperative it is to let go before you continue on this journey towards healing.

That woman robbed me of 6 months of my life. 6 months that I will never get back. 6 months that I could have spent healing. Instead, I was robbed of my peace and of my time.

Don't make the same mistake that I made.

I don't care what you've done, and it doesn't matter what they've done to you. If you can't forgive, it's best to let go altogether. You're just prolonging the inevitable. You're tarnishing what you've had with that person if you can't forgive but still try to remain in each other's lives. So stop waiting, and let's move on.

3.3 - Break The Chain

Let go of the chains that hold you back. The chains that won't let you move towards healing. This journey is long, we've already discussed this. But know that if you hold on to all that baggage, all that hurt, all those dead dreams, you won't get much further. Break the chains of disappointment, of bitterness, of hatred. All those things are a burden that is too heavy for you to carry. And quite frankly, there's no room for those on our journey towards healing. Leave the chains behind. Leave your old life behind. Let's keep walking. Let's keep going.

3.4 - They Weren't Perfect

One strategy that will help you let go of the person you used to share a life with is by reminding yourself of who they really were. When we fall in love, we often end up idolizing the other person. This transcends into the breakup and all of a sudden, we're stuck thinking we just lost the best person in the world. Often times, this is not the case. No matter how good they were, they weren't perfect. They weren't the best thing that ever happened to you, not by a long shot. Love will cloud your judgment. Remember who they were, remember what they did and what they didn't do. To let them go, to move on and heal correctly, it is imperative that you view them for what they truly were.

All the flaws and imperfections. Remind yourself of all the times you two fought, the lies, and the mistrust. Remind yourself of all the things that you hated about them but overlooked because you were too busy loving someone who couldn't love you back the same way.

Remind yourself of the constant indecisiveness, and their inability to make you feel secure in the relationship. Remind yourself of all that you've had to comprise because you two just couldn't see eye to eye. The bad habits, and the baggage you two had.

Despite what they may tell everyone, they weren't perfect, and they certainly weren't better than you.

When we lose someone we genuinely care for, we have this terrible tendency to put that individual on an invisible pedestal. We glorify them and think we'll never find anyone better.

The truth is, they were flawed just like you and I. They had their fair share of problems. You were just too blind to see those flaws because you were in love. Love does that, it blinds you from what is real.

Sit down and make a list of all the things that you hated about this person. You need to really think from an objective perspective.

This isn't to vilify them; instead, all you're doing is rinsing yourself of this belief that they were somehow perfect and flawless. This is how you let them go. This is how you move on. This is how you heal.

3.5 - The Myth of "The One"

In order to let go of the heartbreak, we need to let go of the person who caused it. We do this by first debunking the notion that somehow, they were "the one" for you. I have some sad news for you my friend; if they were the one, they'd still be there. If they were the one, they wouldn't have left, and they sure as heck wouldn't have moved on with someone else in a matter of weeks. No, I'm afraid they're not the one for you. Maybe they were right for you while you two were together. But something happened. Something changed. Now, they're clearly not the one.

I know you love them, and I know you want to believe that what the two of you had was special. That it was real, it was raw. That's what you're telling yourself, right? "How could she move on so quickly, I thought what we had was special?" "How could he just walk away?"

The reality of things is that just because it was special to you, doesn't mean it was special to them. Clearly, it couldn't have been that special. Why? Because they are no longer there, are they?

Think about all the positive memories you two shared, all the good things, all the things that made your relationship feel so 'special.' Now tell me how many of those things were planned, organized, and set into motion by you? Be honest with yourself here. How much positive effort and energy did you put into that relationship, and how much did you receive in return?

Chances are, all these fantastic moments with that other person were only happening because of you. You planned those trips, you did little surprises for them, you spoiled them, showing them affection, planned romantic getaways, and movie dates. You made that relationship special, not the other person. You made the relationship special because they were special to you. Unfortunately, that doesn't always mean that they reciprocate those feelings for you.

You've loved hard and want to fight harder for the belief that they were "the one," I get it. But this is a battle you cannot win.

Let go of the idea that they were somehow perfect because they weren't. Let go of the illusion that they were the one for you. Because they weren't, and they aren't.

All the things that you thought were true about this person; you need to realize that they are no longer relevant. Maybe they were accurate at one point in your relationship, but the truth is that the person that you once fell in love with is no longer there. They aren't the same, and they never will be. Let them go.

3.6. Closure

Closure is an interesting intricate. Everyone seems to have their own opinion about it. What it is and how to get it. Closure helps us accept the worst of things. It enables us to make peace with what is happening. It's putting the questions to rest. The constant wondering, the doubt, the holding back. But the truth is, often times we look for closure in all the wrong places. Closure, as vital as it is for our healing process, has to be obtained by non-other than ourselves.

No one else can give you closure. Not your friends, not your therapist, and least of all, not your ex. You need to make your own closure. You need to come to realize that this is happening, whether you like it or not. Put the quest for answers to rest. Bury it and never seek it again.

I know you want answers. I know you want it to make sense. All the hurt you've been through, the only way you could possibly justify it is with receiving closure from them, right? But you will never find closure in the eyes of someone else. Certainly not the person who broke you. I need you to put to rest the desire to receive closure from someone else. You will not like where you end up when you chase someone else for closure. Make your own closure. Better yet, be your own closure. You do not need anyone else on this road to healing. The quicker you realize this, the quicker you can heal.

3.7 Reminder Purge

Before we embarked on this long journey towards deep healing, I told you one undoubted truth. I told you that this would be incredibly hard and painful. This process will take every ounce of you to accomplish. Now we're moving towards the part where we have to remember to forget. We said it's time to let go. So there you are, you've accepted that this is happening, you're ready to let go, ready to move forward. But how exactly do you do it? Well, you start with the reminder purge. You get rid of everything that reminds you of the heartbreak.

You start with all physical possessions, everything that reminds you of them. The pictures, the clothes that they left behind, the gifts, everything. You take it and throw it all away. This may seem harsh, but you must get rid of it if you want to heal wholeheartedly.

I struggled with this concept for a very long time. It took me over 6 months to finally throw away all that what reminded me of my last relationship. The ironic thing was that everything in my room that reminded me of her, I got myself. The picture frames, photo albums of us, souvenirs, and certain clothing items. I brought all of that into my place. As I cleaned out all of the stuff that haunted me, I finally realized how one-sided that relationship had really been.

I couldn't even look at the pictures before throwing them away. I literally had to rip them up from the back and throw them straight into the trash. This person didn't care about me, put me through hell, and I couldn't even bring myself to look at pictures of her. The power this woman had over me. I knew it had to end. So I threw it all away. Every last piece of her existence eradicated from my life. It was incredibly hard, but it was profoundly easier than to hold on to those memories and realize that you are looking at a stranger. That perhaps you never truly knew them the way you thought you did.

So I'm urging you to get rid of all of their physical belongings. I know this is hard to do, but it's something that must be done.

3.8 - (User) Will No Longer Be Able to Message You

After you have cleansed yourself of their physical memories. It is time to turn to social media. This is where things get complicated.

In this day and age, everyone is so connected. You're going to have to disrupt that connection if you ever want to truly let go and heal.

So delete AND block them on every social media platform you have. Twitter, Facebook, Instagram, Snapchat. After you finish blocking them, you either unfollow all of their close friends, or you mute them. That way, there is no chance that you'll "accidentally" stumble across a story or post where your ex is mentioned. If this seems extreme, it's because it is. There are no half measures when it comes to this. If you commit to healing, then commit! Delete and block them from every social media platform. Then block their email. Yeah, you thought I'd forget about that one huh? I told you, I've been where you've been. I've walked this journey. Delete and block their number on your phone. Leave no trace of their existence behind. You will have time to appreciate the good memories you two shared, but not right now, not while you're healing. This is the time to be fierce.

You have to do this, as much as it hurts you. As much as you don't want to. But that's precisely why you need to do it. Keep going, keep walking, We aren't done yet.

3.9 - How Not To Heal

This book is about teaching you how to heal. How to become whole again. This book is here to guide you when your spirit is crushed. We talked about some fundamental aspects of the healing process. But if I tell you about all the ways to heal, I also have to tell you about all the ways not to heal.

The journey towards deep healing is one that will change the way you do life, it changes everything. But you need to heal the right way, the proper way.

I see it all the time. In fact, I've lived it. People get out of relationships, and they try and numb their pain with alcohol, drugs, and sex. And while that may temporarily fill that void inside your chest. It will never truly make you whole. Do you feel better after a night of drinking? Do you seem happier the morning after that one-night stand? Do the aftereffects of your drug trip make you feel great?

No, they do not. At that very moment, it may alleviate the pain. But truth be told; you're never going to heal if you result to those external escape routes. Don't do it.

3.10 - Toxic Coping Mechanism

My therapist once told me that we all cope differently with grief and loss. And while that is true, yes, we all deal uniquely with loss, one thing remains constant, the way we need to heal to truly overcome our trauma. The trauma might be different from person to person, but the way we overcome that trauma should not be different.

So regardless of what stage of your healing phase you are in, it's essential to understand that healing the right way is crucial in this life. And it doesn't matter if you do everything else right in this book. You can accept their loss, let them go, forgive them, yet if you result in toxic coping mechanisms to numb the pain, to forget, you're not genuinely healing. And you never will.

Don't resort to sex and alcohol. Don't resort to drugs. And don't rush back into the next relationship. That is the worst thing that you could possibly do. It is so easy to want to grab the closest hand you see when you're drowning in pain and suffering. But I am telling you that you'd be wrong to grab that hand. Seeking the company of someone else for the sole purpose of avoiding your own solitude is one of the worst things you could possibly do on this journey. It's detrimental to healing. This is the time in your life to be alone. To listen to your own heart. To nurture yourself. This is the time in your life to put yourself first. Jumping from one failed relationship to another just to avoid the heartbreak is the worst thing you can do for yourself. You're better than that. Don't ever think that happiness in life is tied to another human being. To heal means to understand that simple fact.

Part 4 [Ready for Battle]

4.1 - Turn The Light On

Healing from heartbreak is hard. Incredibly hard, in fact. The longer the relationship was with the person, the longer and harder the process will take. This is completely normal. Don't be surprised, and don't be afraid.

To make it through the path of deep healing and in turn, moving on, we need to first understand that getting over a heartbreak is like fighting a war. Every day, every minute, every hour, you will have emotions, feelings, and thoughts hammering inside your head. Your mind will be a terrible place to be for a very long time. I am here to tell you that you need to prepare yourself for that constant battle. The battle for what you'll want to do, and what you'll need to do. Those two ideas will at first, be completely opposite of each other. But you need to do what is right in order to heal.

I've learned that my most significant help in getting over my heartbreak and disappointment has been creating and defining a relationship with God. I was never a true believer until I got pushed into the deepest waters of despair. I almost drowned in my own sorrows. I almost didn't make it. Truth be told, there was a time where I didn't think I could live for much longer with what I was feeling inside of me. I didn't know how anyone could. I was broken, shattered into a million pieces. On the verge of giving up. But there in my darkest moment, I found him who resuscitated me and brought me back to life. God turned the light on when all I saw was darkness.

The battle wasn't finished, I knew I'd have many months ahead of me to truly overcome this grief that I was carrying in my chest. But something changed. Something happened. Surely my circumstances didn't change, no. They stayed the same; but me? I changed. I finally had someone by my side who'd walk this long journey with me. I found God, and ever since that day, my life has never been the same. The battle wasn't over, but the game changed. I finally had the support I needed to win this war. I found the strength in Jesus Christ, and with him on my side, who could be against me? How could I lose this battle if I had the greatest fighter the world has ever known on my side?

I found the protective armor that I needed to withstand the blows this war would strike me with. In God, I found my weapon to win this war.

I urge you in your quest for healing, to seek out the one thing that can truly make a difference in this journey. Wrestle with God, and there in your darkest hour, you will find who you were always meant to be. You'll find your purpose. You'll find out why you ended up on this road.

On my journey towards deep healing, God's guidance has been the most significant help. I would not be writing this if it wasn't for him. I know that for a fact. I'm not trying to force you into believing in God and all of a sudden, becoming this religious person. You have to make that decision on your own. I would just urge you to keep an open mind.

4.2 - Check Your Circle

As mentioned earlier, this is the part of our journey towards healing, where we will face the most resistance. We're at war here, our mind and heart are in a constant battle that will push us to the very brink of existence. Putting our faith in God and that there will be better days ahead is crucial if we want to keep this fight alive. The battle to survive. But we need something else. Something that will help us immensely. We need to check our circle. Take a step back and look at the people that you talk to daily. Are those people helping you become better? Do their visions align with yours? Do they support you, sharpen you to becoming the best version of yourself? Do they nourish you, inspire you to be great? Because that is what you need, not only on the journey towards healing but rather in life in general. You need those people to have your back, especially when you're on your knees fighting to see another day.

You need to have the right allies to win this war. I had to learn this lesson the hard way. I realized that I had many so-called 'friends' in my life. But when things turned south in my relationship when I lost myself, lost the person that I loved, I was left with nothing. No one to have my back, no one to listen to. People were there when things were good. They would call me when they wanted to party and go out at night. But no one called me to see how I was doing. I knew then that I needed to check my circle and reevaluate who I would call a true friend. Because true friends support you no matter what.

You don't need to have 10-15 friends. No, all you need are 2-3 genuinely good people on this journey, and you're heading in the right direction.

Then, and only then do you have what it takes to win this battle. Check your circle and clean your house. It doesn't matter if you've known them for 10-15 years, if they don't add value to your life, let them go. You don't need dead weight on this journey, you don't need people in your life who will hold you back. What you need are people who will push you forwards, out of this terrible darkness and into the light. Not drag you down any more in-depth than you already are.

You need to set your life on fire and seek those people in your life that will fan your flames. Those flames will set your past on fire, eradicating your mistakes and regrets. Those flames will light the way for a better tomorrow. Those flames will give you purpose and provide you with hope.

4.3 - Seek Help

Having a relationship with God is incredibly important on this journey for healing. If you ask me, it's the most crucial aspect of the healing process. Surrounding yourself with the right people is imperative for your overall wellbeing. They will push you on your darkest days, encourage you when you can't find the strength to get up in the morning. All that is essential. But there is a chance that you need something else. An extra push. A place, a person to confide your darkest fears in.

I'm here to tell you that it is okay to seek help. To find someone to talk to. Someone who's completely unbiased, and has no judgment. I found that talking to a therapist can be an immense help in overcoming grief and loss. And as a man, it is hard for me to admit that speaking to a stranger about my problems can, in fact, be of some relief. But it has helped me become better. Talking to my therapist has helped me let go of a lot of heartache and disappointment.

No matter where you are on your journey towards healing, try and find someone to talk to about your problems. I promise you, when you walk out of that office, you will not feel the same way as when you walked in. A burden will have been lifted. An incredible difficulty.

If you feel like you're too uncomfortable with the idea of pouring your heart out to a complete stranger, then that's even more of a reason to go. I told you that this journey will be uncomfortable. I wasn't lying. It is painful. But it's supposed to be this way. Walkthrough the pain, and walk through the unknown. Take that leap of faith. Talk to someone. There's no shame in showing your weakness and showing your flaws. Your mental health is paramount and shouldn't be neglected. Your mind is the battleground for this war, the battle towards healing. Take care of yourself.

4.4 - Stay Busy

I already told you that on our road to healing, we will be facing a devastating war. A war that needs to be fought on many fronts. We talked about walking this journey with God, surrounding ourselves with the right people, and seeking the help of a therapist to get our deepest feelings off our chest. But now it's your time to kick the gear in extra drive. I'm going to need you to stay busy, stay focused. Don't let your thoughts wander. Stay occupied. Write, read, workout. I'm not saying run from your feelings, rather the opposite. I want you to face them. But it's easy to lose motivation, to just want to lay in bed all day and watch Netflix for 10 hours straight. And while that is okay to do at first, that isn't a viable state to be in for any prolonged period.

Don't lay in your misery. Get up and do something. Seize the day. Use that pain and suffering as a catalyst for change. This is what healing is all about. It's not about returning to your previous state. Healing is about growth; it's about becoming better than ever before. Stay busy, stay active, stay moving.

4.5 - Not Going Back

Look how far we've come on this journey. We covered some ground. A lot of progress and self-reflection. This is what it's supposed to be like. You're heading in the right direction. We both are. But no matter how much progress we've made, there will be times when someone or something is going to try and pull you back.

I'm here to tell you that you cannot let it do that. We aren't going back. Ever. There is no going back to your old life. I know you will be tempted. We, humans, love the familiar, the past, the comfortable. But I am telling you that things can't just go back to "how they were." Because there is no back and there never can be. Life only moves forward. Stop trying to go back, or you will always be disappointed. You will never read this book for the first time again. You can revisit this page later. But it's already a memory.

For a very long time, I've tried to get back with someone who, for better or worse, had no business in being in my life anymore. I wanted to keep them in my life and start over with them. Because I loved that person more than anything in this world. I quickly came to the realization that it doesn't matter how much you change, how much you become better, how much you grow, you can never go back to how things used to be. The person that I knew, the person that I fell in love with, died a long time ago. I was just too blind to see it in my quest for my old life.

I know that you think that things can go back to how they were before, but I am telling you from the bottom of my heart that they can't. You can't go back. Not to the partner who broke you into a million pieces. Not to your old life, toxic friends, bad habits. We're not going back to any of that. If we want to truly heal and genuinely become whole again, we need to fight the urge to want to go back.

Every morning tell yourself these words:" I AM NOT GOING BACK."

Every single day. Say it, mean it, live it. Our old life is dead and gone. It is time to step into your new life. A better one. Keep your head up high and walk towards healing.

Part 5 [Remind Yourself Of Who You Are]

5.1 - Recover Who You Are

When you get into a relationship, everything changes. When you fall in love, even more changes. Their wants become your wants, their needs end up being your needs. Their identity becomes entangled with yours. "I's" turn into "we's." You stop thinking about yourself and think about them. All the time. When you fall in love, it is easy to put yourself second and your partner ahead of your own needs and wants. It happens all the time.

Often times, we don't even realize that it is happening. You know when you walk into a clothing store, and you immediately look to the women's section and think to yourself: "Wow, this would really look good on her." It happens unconsciously. It becomes second nature. It certainly did for me.

This continues on and on, as long as the relationship lasts. The longer the relationship, the deeper the connection and dependency will usually run. And when its finally all said and done, when the relationship has run its course, you find yourself lost, like something is missing. What's missing is your partner. But with them being gone, another thing is also missing; part of your own identity. That is why, often after a breakup, we find ourselves feeling lost and empty. Because we didn't just lose our partner, we lost part of ourselves.

For months and often years, we spent so much time figuring out what someone else needed, that we totally neglected our own needs and wants. And when that person is no longer in our life, we feel like we lost who we were. We don't know who we are anymore with them being gone.

I am telling you that now it is time to figure out who you are without them. Remind yourself of who you were before they crashed into your life. Remember what you wanted out of life. Remember what your hopes and dreams were. Remember where you wanted to go to grad school. Remember what your favorite color was, not theirs. Remember what your favorite food was, not theirs. Remind yourself of all the good things that are happening in your life without them. Pull their existence out of your identity. Replace the 'we' with "I." Replace their dreams with yours; their hopes and goals with your desires and goals.

This is a process that will take many months. It's an unlearning. When you truly love someone, I mean unapologetically love someone, they grow into the roots of you. They become part of you. You have to pull them out. Eradicate their sheer existence from within you.

You have to shower them out of your hair. Scrub their fingerprints from your skin, rinse yourself from their smell, their memory, and their presence.

You have to cleanse yourself from their presence. Leave no trace behind. Some days you'll spend 45 minutes in the shower just to rinse yourself off from a single memory the two of you shared. So many tears will stream down your face into the tub, you won't know whether they're your actual tears or merely the water from the showerhead. You won't really know, and you won't care. There will be days where you'll scream so loudly, your lungs will feel like they're about to be set on fire.

It's okay to breakdown. To feel like you've lost everything, lost yourself.

You have to come to terms with the fact that you let them leave with so many pieces of you. You have to forgive yourself for loving yourself thin, for forgetting about your dreams because you were so busy trying to save someone who didn't want to be saved.

You're not weak for breaking down, you're human. This, too, is part of the healing process. Don't think this pain will last forever, because it won't.

5.2 - Reinvent Yourself

Remembering who you were before they came into your life and working your way toward becoming that person again is only half the battle. Don't just stop at remembering who you were before, it's time to reinvent yourself. Healing isn't just about becoming whole again; deep, genuine healing will make you want to become better than ever before. You'll be stronger and wiser. At the end of this journey towards healing, there won't be the old you. No, that old you is dead and gone. You can never replicate that version of yourself. And you shouldn't want to. There are two types of pain. Pain that breaks you and pain that changes you. This pain that you're feeling now; do not let it break you. Instead, let it turn you into becoming the best version of yourself.

Life is about growth, not stagnancy. It's time to go above and beyond. It's time to reinvent yourself, to become the highest version of yourself. It's time sharpen yourself, to be reborn out of the despairs of yesterday. Like a phoenix rising out of its ashes, I'll need you to rise; this time higher than you've ever been before.

Every transformation always gets worse before it gets better. It's supposed to be that way. But when it goes up, it goes higher than it has ever been before.

I know that you're struggling with finding who you are because, for years, you believed you'd have that other person next to you by your side. Your person. They were supposed to be there. But when you look around you now, all you see is loneliness. They left. And with them gone, you feel utterly lost and hopeless. I know that feeling. Trust me, I've been there. But I promise you that you're more than a partner. More than a boyfriend or girlfriend, husband or wife. You're not defined by your relationship status. I know that after years of being with someone, that can feel odd to you because your identity has tied itself to that other person. And now that they're gone, you're struggling to find yourself, yet alone reinvent yourself. I get it. But you need to let go of the mindset that they completed you. You were complete before they came into your life, and you're still complete now that they're gone. I know it doesn't feel like it because you're lost. But you will find your way back home again. I promise you. Just keep walking, I'm here for you. I'm walking this journey with you.

5.3 - Find your Passion

Healing, as painful as it is, as dark, heartbreaking, and uncomfortable as it may be, it is also one of the most beautiful experiences we human beings can endeavor. There are times where we don't just get broken, but instead, we get utterly destroyed. Shattered to the point of dust. When things break into a hundred pieces, at least you still have the chance to put those pieces back together, right? There's hope. But what happens if we get so hurt, so disappointed, that our life simply turns into dusk and ashes. All our hopes, our dreams, our goals are destroyed right in front of our eyes. All we have left is dust, broken dreams, and broken promises.

We want to go back and edit the story, so it has a different ending. We want to repair this heartbreak. We just want to make it right. But what if God has other plans for us? What if he doesn't want to bring us back to what was known to us? What if God desires to make something completely brand new with these ashes that once reflected what our life used to look like? What if this time, something greater is meant to be created? We automatically think that the shattering of our dreams and hopes couldn't possibly be used for something good. But what if the shattering of our lives is the only way to get dust back to its basic form so that something new can be made? We can look at the dusk as a result of an unfair breaking. Or we can see dust as a crucial ingredient for something truly great. Something better. Something new.

Dust doesn't have to signify the end. Dust is often what must be present for a new beginning. On your path towards healing, your goal shouldn't just be whole again. Your goal shouldn't be to just be the old you. This is the time in your life to reinvent yourself. To find your passion. Find your love for life.

You do this by paying more attention to what stirs your heart. Pay attention to the music that makes your soul spark. Pay attention to

63

how your eyes react to the possibility of new places to travel to. Pay attention to the things that make you laugh, the things that make you smile. Really focus on figuring out what compels you. Really focus on discovering the aspects of the world that interest you, challenge you, and make you want to learn and grow. You have to pay attention to the little things. Because those little things are what make you, you. Those little things are the building blocks of your future.

You've spent so much of your time merely focusing on what someone else wanted from you. What their dreams were, how to make them happy. How to satisfy their needs. You spent so much of your energy being exactly who they needed, and now it is time to figure out precisely what you need and what you want. It's time to pay attention to the calling of your own heart; it's time to nurture yourself.

Find your passion, find something that you've always wanted to do in this world, but never did because you were too afraid or too busy. You're alone now, this is the time to be selfish. To work on yourself, for yourself. No one else to hold you back. No one to distract you from your true calling.

The path towards deep healing lies in your understanding of who you are. Who do you see when you look in the mirror? More importantly; who do you want to be?

Do you want to be a photographer? Then be a photographer. Get yourself a camera and start taking pictures. Do you want to be a writer? Then write. Today. Not tomorrow, not next week, not when you're feeling better. Now. Whatever it is that intrigues you, that gets your heart going; you chase that down. And nothing else, no one else. No matter how small or how big that dream or passion of yours is, you pursue it and conquer it. Life is too short to not go for the things that make you, you.

We've established that healing is one of the most excruciating things we can go through, but I am here to tell you that it's also one of the most beautiful times in your life. Where there is death in endings, there is also new life to be found. New beginnings.

By new beginnings, I don't necessarily mean with other people. Not right away. I mean new beginnings with yourself. Finding out what makes you tick is an incredible journey. One that will take a lifetime. But on your path towards healing, you will quickly realize how powerful the quest for finding one's passion can be.

This journey that you are on, it's yours; yours alone. I'm here to guide you, but ultimately you have to embrace it on your own. I can't tell you what your passion is. Only you can do that.

5.4 - What's On Your Bucket-List

I want you to do something for me. I want you to take out a piece of paper and write down all the things that you want to do in this life. All your dreams and wishes. We call this the bucket-list. We all have one in our heads. But how many of us actually pursue the items on our list? Write down all the places you've always wanted to travel to. Write down the hobbies that you always said you'd pick up but never got around to do. The languages you wanted to learn. Maybe learning how to finally dance. Going skydiving or wakeboarding. Whatever it is, write it down. Take your time and really think about it. You may be surprised to see how many things you've wanted to do. It could be 10 items, it could be 100 items. The more, the better. Some will be harder to do than others, but the goal is to have plenty of options.

Once you've finished writing that list, take a step back, give yourself some time to think, and come back to it later. Maybe you'll think about a few more things that you really want to do. Add it all to the list. No goal is too big or too small. After you've finished, go over all those things on that list. How many did you find? 15? 20? It's crazy how many dreams we really have when we take a second and think about what WE want. Not what our partner wants, not what our parents want, not what our boss wants. But instead what WE want.

This is what healing is all about, it's about finding your passion, finding the things in this world that make your heart skip a beat.

And don't be too hard on yourself for not completing any of those bucket-list goals earlier on in your life. There's no room to dwell on the past on this path to healing. Remember, we are not going back. Only forward. So decide that today is the day. Today is the day where you finally put yourself first!

I want you to hang that list up somewhere where you'll see it every day. In your room, next to your door, on your bathroom mirror. Wherever it is, just look at it every day. And I want you to set an obtainable goal for yourself.

Don't categorize your items on the list, either. Your dreams are far too big and too complicated to be put into a box or category. Write as you please, all over the paper.

Then tell yourself that every month, you'll find a way to check off at least one of those items on your list. Some months you'll be able to do 2 or 3. But shoot for at least one goal a month. It could be something small like waking up early and seeing the sun come up at the beach. It could be something big like traveling to Australia and learning how to surf. The size of the goal doesn't necessarily matter; what matters is that it is your goal.

We are at a point in our healing process, where it is time to be selfish. Time to put yourself first. Time to reinvent yourself. You do this by listening to your heart, and finding out what your dreams are, what your hopes are.

It is astonishing how often we put our dreams on hold, simply because we are too occupied with trying to create dreams with someone else. Someone who has no business in even dreaming with us. But those days are over; it's time to create your bucket list and check things off of that list. Week after week. This is your journey, your life. Make sure you live it how you want to live it.

5.5 - Self-Improvement

The path of deep healing is one that is rooted in self-improvement. Take that pain and hurt and let it help you become the best version of yourself. This is the time in your healing process, where you really need to listen to yourself. Look at your life and ask yourself:" Am I happy with my current situation? Am I satisfied with the people I surround myself with? Am I happy with my career path, my school, my ideology"? On the other side of brokenness, lies a world full of new beginnings. The death to one world means the beginning of a new one. A fresh start. A new beginning.

This beginning is a sign. It's time to step into your calling. Who do you want to be in this world, and who are you tired of being? Life is about evolving, life is about growth. Often times, when we end up in the wrong kind of relationships, we tend to become stagnant. Instead of improving and becoming better, we often tend to stay the same, or we end up becoming more flawed.

Look back at your relationship and try and analyze all the times where you acted out of behavior. A situation occurred, and you handled it poorly. Maybe you were too jealous, too insecure, or too harsh. Don't beat yourself up over your past mistakes. Instead, think about how you could have handled that situation differently, and then learn from it. Make sure you don't make the same mistake again the next time you find yourself in a similar situation with someone else. The goal of healing is to become better for yourself. And that will directly impact the people around you. That way, you can be better for others. That is real growth. Don't go through all this grief and heartache just to, later on, make the same mistakes again.

Self-Improvement is self-awareness. Look at yourself and think about all the things that you do not like about yourself. No one is perfect, not you, not me. But what are some toxic traits that may have negatively affected your last relationship? Maybe you were too clingy, too jealous, too insecure. There is no shame in admitting to any of that. The journey to deep healing is one that looks at oneself and analyses what behaviors need to be changed and what qualities need to be nourished. For there is an immense amount of good in you, there is without a doubt also some bad in you. Flaws that can and should be corrected. Life is about growth. Healing is about growth. Therefore in life, we always will be subject to healing. As we should. You should want to become better each and every single day.

5.6 – Travel

No matter where you are on your path to healing, I highly encourage you to travel. Travel as far as you can, as often as you can. Travel by yourself. There is nothing quite like it. When you distance yourself from everything familiar, remove yourself from all that is the norm, that is when you genuinely get in touch with yourself. The real you. Who you are is more visible sitting in a café, 3,000 miles away from home, than when you're at home, stuck in the same routine. Who you are, becomes evident when you're on a layover halfway across the world. When you take out all the noise from your daily life. Remove your school, your work, your social life. Leave all those things at the gate before boarding the plane.

When you travel, there is no room for distractions. Not when you're on your path towards healing. You have enough of a burden to carry. Find the time to get away from it all.

I love to travel. Heartbroken or not. But there is something about traveling when you're broken. Broken beyond repair. It's raw, it's real. You feel everything so much more. You get lost in your own thoughts. The pain, the disappointment, the vulnerability. It's all right there. There's no hiding from it. No escaping it. Things sound so much different when you travel too. The announcement the gate agent makes when boarding the flight. The clicking your seatbelt makes when buckling up in your tiny economy seat. The takeoff sounds different as well, feels different. You're moving at 300 miles down the runway, yet as you look outside the window, you realize that time somehow ends up standing still. You part ways with the city, with the person that crushed your soul.

You'll think the distance between the two of you will make things easier. Out of sight, out of mind. But if you've ever been in love, I mean really in love, you know that it isn't that simple. Far from it.

It'll get easier, but not now, not at this very moment. Now is when the real journey begins. No matter how far you travel, you'll see that person. At the corner store in Paris. The beach club in Bali. The museum in Sydney. The restaurant in Barcelona. No matter where you go, there they'll be. Their smell, their laughter, their tears, their memory will haunt you to the ends of this earth. But that is precisely the point. If you want genuine healing, you don't run from your problems and pain. You embrace them.

I actually just left Bali as I'm writing this. I love Bali, it holds a special place in my heart. But one thing about Bali is that it is filled with so many memories of me and my last relationship. The woman that I've adored for years, her memories are still very much alive on this island. We spent almost two weeks there for our birthdays.

So many incredible memories we've made there. To now go back to that place without her has been heart-wrenching. But as hard as returning to this place without her has been, it has also been necessary to remind myself that even though she is no longer in my life, life still goes on. Yes, she's gone, and I will never see her again. But that doesn't mean that my life stops moving. I mentioned earlier that in order to truly heal from heartbreak, you need to become profoundly uncomfortable. How do you think I felt visiting the same beaches, restaurants, and bars that she and I have visited in the past? I saw her everywhere. Her laughter, her smile, her jokes, her attitude. Being there, this time was a constant reminder that the world I once knew, no longer exists. That life is gone. But just because our time together ended doesn't mean that the places we've visited lost their magic. If anything, I was reminded that a life without her, still entails mesmerizing sunsets and exhilarating mornings.

Traveling helps, and I urge you to do it often and unapologetically.

I know you're hurting. I know you're scared. Scared that this pain will never subside. Scared that you'll never find true happiness again. Scared that you are damaged goods. That you're not good enough. You're scared that you can never climb out of this abyss.

But I am here to tell you that you can, and you will. You must. Fear is self-imposed. Meaning it doesn't exist. In only lives in your head. It's an intangible. You created it, and you can destroy it too. In fact, you're the only one that can. If you face your fear of never finding happiness again, you can overcome it. Face your heartbreak, face your disappointment. Face your hurt. And only then will you beat it. Not only did you beat it back. That energy is never lost. That negative energy, that fear that hurt, is destroyed. It comes back as confidence, as resilience, as hope.

Now with this battle won, you're going to think to yourself:" What else am I capable of? What else am I holding back? What am I running from that I don't need to? What else can I overcome?"

You face that fear of loneliness, and you become the person you truly need to be.

Traveling helps you to become that person. It enables you to find yourself.

I've been to many places on this beautiful earth. Ironically enough, some of my favorite trips have been under the worst circumstances. I was broken beyond repair only twice in my life. At least, speaking from a romantic perspective. And each trip that followed those heartbreaks had brought me closer towards my destiny. Those trips helped me become whole again. Whether that was Iceland, Australia, South Africa, or now Bali again. Each of these places had helped me find my way back home when I was utterly lost.

Driving around the countryside of Iceland in the dead of winter, helped me obtain a different kind of peace. It helped me ignite a love for my own solitude. On the other hand, my relationship with God began when I went to Australia. I found out who I was always meant to be. Shark-diving in South Africa made me feel alive when there was a point in my life that I felt dead inside. Each destiny, each trip, each place I've traveled to, has helped me heal in a way that wouldn't have otherwise been possible for me to do if I hadn't jumped on that plane.

There are times in life where you have to leave home to find your way back home. Sometimes you need to get lost, to be found again. On your journey towards healing, you will find out that time in your life has arrived. It's time to get lost, my friend. It's time to leave home.

5.7 - Make a Difference

I've noticed that on my own personal journey towards healing from heartbreak and disappointment, one thing that has helped me the most was to serve and help others. This may seem counterintuitive to many because there you are; broken, let down, weak, and alone. How could you possibly help others when you can't even help yourself? That is precisely the point. The way to forget about your own pain is to help other people, so you forget about your own grief.

A few months back, right in the middle of my heartbreak when I was at my lowest, I decided to volunteer at my church. They have these community outreaches every few months where you help others. You give back. So a dear friend of mine encouraged me to go with her and so I did. It was honestly one of the best days I've ever had.

We visited a facility that takes care of adults with specific mental and physical disabilities. People from all walks of life. Men and women. They all had their own personal story, but the one thing that they all had in common was their past misfortune. Many of these people were abused as children, lost their parents, or sustained another severe trauma. Add to the fact that many of these people are mentally impaired, and you'd think these people are miserable and hate life. But after being there for just a few minutes, I quickly realized how happy they were with doing the smallest things.

We built a puzzle, plaid basketball, threw tennis balls around, and had lunch together. You'd be hard-pressed to find any kids today who would willingly participate in those activities, let alone enjoy them. But there, those people loved every moment. They have so many problems that they are dealing with, and which caused them devasting pain, yet they get excited about a simple basketball match. Those people have learned to enjoy the little things. It really puts things into perspective when you witness this firsthand.

For that one hour that we were there, I completely forgot about my own problems, my own pain. Because there I was, helping people who were of so much worse off than me. I loved every moment of it. That day I realized that the path towards healing is one that involves generosity; it requires kindness; it includes selfless acts.

Often times, we not only go through pain and heartbreak to grow ourselves, and to get better ourselves; but also to help others who are in desperate need of help and perhaps advice. Over this past year, I've written dozens of articles on life, pain, self-improvement, and relationship advice. All with the foundation of my own experience that I have gone through. My work has been shared and viewed by hundreds of people. And I've gotten so much feedback from some of those people who were positively impacted by my words and encouragement. People who were going through similar circumstances and needed that advice.

I quickly realized that I could make a difference, that this may very well be my purpose. And if out of a hundred people, it helps just one person, then I've completed my mission. I've made a difference in someone's life. And that my friend is the greatest gift you can give in this world. To help someone else without gaining a single thing in return, that is pure happiness.

The only way I could share my painful experiences was by walking the journey myself. How can I give advice if I've never been the subject of these painful experiences myself? And although I would have never chosen this road nor wish it on my worst enemy, I am thankful for it because it has made me a better man and has led me to help others who are in desperate need of saving.

So stop focusing on yourself, stop blaming yourself, or others for that matter. When you focus too much on your own pain, you lose sight of the true purpose. Your purpose is to make a difference in this world. It may be small, it may be significant. But there is a purpose. Make a difference. Stand tall and be kind, even if the world hasn't always been kind to you. That is what healing is about.

Part 6: [Find Your Peace]

6.1 - Search for Tranquility

The path towards healing requires one to find peace. You can't heal if you are not at peace with yourself. One of the greatest lessons I've learned is that only you can be your own peace. Not your partner, not your friends, not your family. There's a constant war raging all around us, and that war begins from within. Our only hope for peace is to win that war. In this life, there will be many dark days. There will be chaos, hurt, pain, and disappointment. There will be people who try to break you. Some will try to destroy you. To overcome all of those challenges, we first need to find our inner peace from within.

Peace means "harmony, wholeness, completeness, tranquility." To find peace means to experience wholeness. When we find peace, we are made whole. When that heartbreak shattered you and your dreams beyond repair, peace is the gateway to become whole once again. You may have been broken, destroyed, left for dead, but you are not a lost cause. You will be made whole yet. And it starts with finding your own peace. Find your peace, and you'll find wholeness too.

I realized that for me to find genuine peace, I had to seek Jesus. I found my peace in him. Walking on this journey with him has been the greatest gift of my life. He has guided me, protected me, he has lightened the way and given me signs. Strengthened me on my darkest days. There will be trouble in the world, but in him, you'll find peace. I promise you that if you open your heart and let God in, nothing will ever be the same for you. Your situations may not change, but you will. You won't instantly become a man of wealth and riches. But you'll be rich in God's presence and wealthy of his grace.

There will be trouble in this world, there is no way to avoid that. But you can take heart, for he has overcome the world. It doesn't matter what they've done to you. It doesn't matter that they hurt you so badly, you didn't think you could survive it. Understand that God is positioning you. When you come to terms with that fact, you don't lose peace over what people may have done to you, because there is not a single situation that they can put you in, that God won't show up in the midst of. There may be a fire burning all around you. That grief that you can't seem to shake off is consuming you. But in that fire, there will be someone else standing with you. He will be by your side. That fire can be excruciatingly hot, way hotter than what you imagined it would be. But rest assured that you will find peace in Jesus. The only thing that is going to fall off in that fire is the ropes that had you bound. God wants you to be in the fire to set you free. To bring you peace.

It is impossible to experience peace if you're expecting perfection. To live in peace, you have to surrender your expectations of perfection. Peace isn't found in a place or person. Peace is not found in a problem-free set of circumstances. It is not that God delivers you out of it, it's that he meets you in it.

I came to realize that nothing in this world will bring you peace if you don't first have peace in your own heart. But even though no situation or person can bring you peace, they certainly can disrupt it. The path towards healing isn't just about finding peace, it's also about eliminating situations and any people that will disturb it. So think about circumstances and people that rob you of your peace. Maybe it's an ex that still reaches out to you whenever they feel vulnerable. Perhaps it's a job that you go to and are extremely unhappy at. No matter what it is, if it costs you your peace, it's a luxury that you can no longer afford. Plain and simple.

Ask yourself this one simple question: "is this disrupting my peace"? If the answer to that question is yes, then it needs to go. No question about it. You cannot heal in an environment that is causing you constant stress. Just like you can't heal an open cut in a dirty environment, you also can't heal your broken heart in a draining and toxic environment.

Free yourself from what is eating away at your peace. Because your peace is the most important thing you have. The world may be a loud and scary place, but inside of you, there has to be peace. A peace so strong and so unshakable that you can stand in a brazing storm, untouched and unfaced.

You cannot know deep healing until you first meet genuine peace.

6.2 - The Best Is Yet To Come

I know that part of the reason why you're so devastated in your loss is that you believe you lost the best thing in your life. Your heart is filled with regret because you messed up a great thing. You think that because you've had some phenomenal times with a certain someone, and now that they are no longer there, you could never trump those times and indeed couldn't possibly find someone 'better.' The simple truth is that we humans are creatures of habit. We love our routine, and we don't like change. We certainly don't like letting go. We long for the past, for the familiar, because we believe that those were our best memories. We think we can't do better.

That's why we don't like letting go of something or someone that is tied to good memories, even if that something or someone is also bound to a lot of bad memories. We try to brush the bad away and only focus on the good. It doesn't matter if that someone lied, abused, and manipulated us for years because we remember that one fantastic weekend where we had an incredible time. Where for 3 days, we had peace. Well, what about the other 28 days?

You're fishing for good memories and avoid all the bad memories. Deep down, you know they weren't right for you, yet you still think you cannot do better. But I am here to tell you that yes, you can do better, and you will.

The truth is, you will never find someone exactly like the person you have lost. That is as equally refreshing, as it is terrifying. They were unique in their own way; flawed, but unique. You can never replace that. And you know what? That is okay because there will be someone out there who will treat you the way you deserve to be treated. They won't be perfect, but they'll be different. It won't be the same, and that's precisely the point.

There's nothing more painful than walking away from what we love before we're ready to. Even when every part of us knows that we must go, we have to walk away from this. Deep down, we know it. But yet we try to linger, we try to hold on. We forget that there is a future. Something about us forgets that there are good things ahead. Even great things. And that is what we must understand in these times of desperation. When we are broken, disappointed, and angry, we have to remind ourselves that all of our best memories aren't all behind us. In fact, the best things are yet to come.

That is what matters. That is what has always mattered. On this road to healing, you have to remind yourself that even when you're surrounded by nothing but darkness, there is light at the end of this journey. Just because the scene in the rearview mirror looks nicer than the current view on the road ahead doesn't mean you'll never reach another beautiful destination. It just means you're not there yet.

You have to believe that there are so, so many better things coming than any of the things that you left in the past. So many new memories and milestones. By yourself and with someone else. You need to have faith in the future, hope that there will be a better tomorrow. That tomorrow may take weeks or months to come, but it'll happen. And when that tomorrow occurs, you'll look back and be awfully proud that you've made it. You persevered.

Look back at some of the worst days of your life. During those times, you, too, thought you would never see another good day. Back then, you also figured you couldn't do better. You thought you couldn't move on from that devastating heartbreak, but guess what? You did. Because that's what you do, you overcome, you endure, you persevere. Because you are stronger than you could ever imagine. So when you look back at some of your worst days, remind yourself that is precisely where you are right now - you're currently enduring some of your worst days. But this season doesn't last. Just like it didn't last back then either. The best is yet to come.

Remember that when you are on your journey towards healing. Have hope, have faith.

Throughout your heartbreak, you will feel like you've lost the best part of you, the best part of your life. When those feelings emerge, you have to take yourself back to the beginning. Take yourself back to the start and remind yourself how unexpectedly you found those people and things that turned out to change your life in such a beautiful way. Remember how suddenly they crashed into your life. Remember? Remember how you two once met. How the universe aligned for the two of you to meet.

You may think that life is unfair right now. But remind yourself of how good life has been to you throughout all these years. It has surprised you for the better many times, and it will continue to do just that. Maybe not today or tomorrow, but one day it will. Life is scary, and it can be awfully confusing. But the real beauty in life is understanding that the best moments are still waiting for you on the other side. You just need to find the courage to take that leap of faith. Take that step toward the unknown, and on the other side, you'll come out healed; you'll come out whole again. Ready for your next beautiful destination.

I know you may think that that you'll never find someone better, but there are over 7 billion people on this planet, do we really want to pretend that there won't be someone else, someone better? You'll find the right person when you stop holding on to the wrong one. You will heal when you realize that the best is yet to come.

6.3 - *Wrong Direction, Redirection*

I have to confess something to you; I am awful at directions. I've been living in Miami for 8 years and still use my GPS for almost anything. I'm not proud of it, but it's the truth. You know what I love about my GPS? No matter how many wrong turns and mistakes I make along the journey, the GPS has a way of correcting the error. It'll say, 'wrong direction – redirecting.' In a female British accent too. I don't know why I changed it to a British female voice, it just sounds reassuring you know.

I think that's a perfect illustration of how God works in our lives. It doesn't matter that you've made 7 wrong turns, he'll guide you towards your right destination. It doesn't matter if you were going in the wrong direction for 20 minutes, or maybe 2 years. Because he'll guide you where you need to go. Before I found Jesus, I didn't know where my life was taking me. I didn't have that sense of security and direction that a GPS provides. Well, except my cell phone of course. My phone helped me get to where I needed to go on my daily activities. But it wasn't until I found Jesus that I finally knew where I needed to go in life. He guided me towards becoming who I was always meant to be. And steered me away from what I thought I wanted at the time. Jesus showed me that I was heading down the wrong path, surrounded by the wrong people.

So, remember that when the next time things don't turn out the way you expected them to and the way you hoped. That God is positioning you. He's redirecting you. Because that relationship you so desperately wanted to stay in was causing you to head in the wrong direction. The rejection that hurt you in a hundred different ways; that was his way of protecting you. By redirecting you. You thought what you had was great, but what if he's preparing you for something even greater?

On your path towards healing, you have to understand that your current and past circumstances, weren't necessarily a punishment. You were heading in the wrong direction, and by finally being removed from that situation, you're now being redirected. This doesn't mean the journey is over. Not by a long shot. But it means you're finally on the right road, heading the right way.

6.4 - Rejection is Gods Protection

I know that right now, it may not seem that way, but rejection isn't necessarily a bad thing. God often will use rejection as a way to protect you. I know this because I am speaking from personal experience. Not too long ago, I found myself in an awfully confusing and painful situation. After an initial breakup occurred between me and someone who meant a great deal to me, I was dragged into what became the longest and most traumatizing 6 months of my life. Her constant back and forth of 'I miss you's' and 'I still need more time's.' Her constant blaming and guilt-tripping, leading me on and giving me hope that there was a future for the two of us. Lies and manipulation. The most toxic environment I have ever been in. And at the end of that disaster, 6 months later, there I was, willing and wanting to continue to fight for this person with the idea that she wanted to that as well. Because well, that's what she told me. It quickly became evident that all that was false,

90

she simply used me as an emotional crutch until she became strong enough to run into the arms of someone else. And that's precisely what she did. In a matter of days. Right after telling me that she still loved me. Calling that 'rejection' would be an understatement.

The reason why I am sharing this personal experience with you is that I need you to understand that just because you want something, doesn't mean it's right for you. That rejection is God's protection.

I wanted to get back with that woman. I prayed to God to restore our relationship and reconnect us. Even after those 6 long months of back and forth, I still wanted her back. What I wanted wasn't in my best interest. She clearly wasn't what I needed. And God knew that. So when I prayed for him to bring her back to me, he probably said something along the lines of: "oh, you want her back? Are you sure? Let me show you who you really are asking to have brought back into your life". And then, instead of doing what I asked him to do, he showed me that person's actual true colors. He showed me who she really was. He opened my eyes. All of a sudden, I saw how foolish I was all those months for not seeing the signs and red flags sooner. I was blind, and he opened my eyes. He answered my prayer, not by giving me what I wanted, but by not giving me what wasn't meant for me.

Rejection is a powerful thing. It hurts, shakes us to our very core. But trust that there lies protection in your rejection. On your own path towards healing, you'll come to understand this too. It might just take a little for you to see it.

6.5 Self-Compassion

On your road towards healing, you have to make sure that you don't beat yourself up over all the mistakes that you've made. Yes, accountability is essential, it's vital if we want to grow from our failures. But making yourself feel bad for messing up isn't going to change anything. You don't want to be too hard on yourself. Accept where you went wrong and move on. It is easy to get stuck in that "how could I be so dumb" mentality. Regret is a disease that eats at your mind and poisons your soul. Do not fall for it. Learn to love yourself because the love you have for yourself will reflect how others will love you. You can't expect others to give you what you cannot give to yourself first. On your road to healing, remember to love yourself, all of you. The flaws, the imperfections, the dysfunctions. You're more than your mistakes. Never let anyone tell you otherwise. No matter who it is.

It is easy to start resenting yourself when you're the one who made irreversible mistakes that caused the end of a relationship. And it's a lot easier to resent yourself when you've been rejected, lied to, abandoned. When the ones we love walk away, we feel inadequate. We think we somehow aren't worthy of love. We believe we aren't good enough, damaged goods even. It's easy to forget about all your good qualities when you've continuously been told all that is wrong with you. It's easy to forget to love yourself when you're too busy loving the wrong person.

On your path towards healing, you have to understand that only you can heal yourself. That is why self-compassion is a vital attribute on this journey. Self-compassions means to kiss yourself, hug yourself, to love yourself. All of you. Remind yourself how much you have to offer. Make a list of all the good qualities you possess. Maybe you're funny, tall, smart, patient, affectionate, understanding, talented, artsy, committed, athletic, fit, whatever it is. It's your positive quality. You may not even know it, but you are unique in your own way. And others will appreciate that. Just because you've been let down and rejected in the past, doesn't mean that there is anything wrong with you. Stop focusing on your shortcomings. Yes you've made mistakes, yes they've lied to you, yes they betrayed your trust, yes you hurt them. Stop loathing yourself for mistakes that happened in the past. You can't undo the past, but you can reinvent yourself for a new future. The kind of future that you want.

To do that, you need to learn self-compassion. Whenever you hear your inner voice talking about regret; stop, pause, and remind yourself of all the good things in your life. Remind yourself of all the good in you. Switch out self-blame for kindness and caring. Your words and thoughts have incredible power. Don't make yourself your worst enemy. Be your own greatest supporter. Don't dim your inner fire with doubt, regret, and self-loathing. Instead, nurture your light with encouragement, self-love, and hope. Erring is part of being human. Acknowledging your mistakes and misfortunes is certainly okay, but that's it, let it be and move on. The journey to deep healing is far too long to be staying stuck in this state of mind that you aren't worthy.

6.6 Self-Love

Self-compassion is a crucial skill one must acquire if healing is to fully happen. As is self-love. In fact, there is no healing without the ability to love yourself. You cannot love someone else if you can't love yourself. And you certainly cannot heal if you don't love who you are. When you're heartbroken, there will be many times when all you feel is pain and disappointment. During those times, the last thing on your mind will be to love yourself, but those are the times when you need to love yourself the most. Yes, that relationship didn't work-out, and I know it sucks. I know it's hard to come to terms with the fact that you woke up in an entirely different world than you may have gone to sleep in. But this is happening, and you need to accept it. Just because someone stopped loving you doesn't mean you should stop loving yourself.

No matter how secure and confident you are, heartbreak has the tendency to shake that security to its very foundation. Heartbreak does just that, it breaks you. And through those cracks, disappointment, resentment, doubt, and insecurities start to slip through. It takes over every single part of you. Every fiber, every thought will be consumed with them. It's like a virus.

It's easy to forget to love yourself when you're fighting to survive this infection. But you have to understand one thing; the only way to beat this vicious disease is through self-love. Let it be your beacon of hope. Let it be a reminder of who you are. The real you. Don't let disappointment, rejection, and regret, tie you down. Self-love will set you free.

You cannot continue on this road towards healing until you can look into the mirror and love who you're looking at. Love yourself unconditionally and irrevocable. Now, in the midst of despair. Not next month, not when you fixed that awful bad habit of yours. Not when you're in a better place. Not when you've found a better job. Not when you're in another relationship. Not when you've moved on. There is no moving on without self-love. Self-love is the one thing in this world that is unconditional. There's no 'I'll love myself tomorrow' no 'I'll love myself if he comes back to me.' None of that. Self-love isn't optional. You owe it to yourself to love yourself.

I know you may think that you have nothing left to give. Nothing left in you to love yourself. You invested so much time, love, and energy into something, someone, just to see that fall apart. You can't possibly fathom to just even give an inch. I know how you feel, trust me, I've been there. That emptiness inside of you, it made itself a home inside of me too. For a very long time, I struggled with it. But I'm telling you that you need to fill that empty void with self-love. You've spent so much time loving yourself thin, all to love someone who didn't deserve your love in the first place. It's time to use all that love and pour it into the one person who deserves it the most; yourself.

You deserve all the love in the world. And it starts with you. If you want to heal, truly heal and become whole again, then part of that wholeness will require self-love. The sooner you realize that the faster you'll be able to recover from your heartbreak.

6.7 - Choose Yourself

Life will be full of choices. What clothes you wear. What you're going to have for lunch. Where you live. Where you work. Who you date. All these are choices that are virtually all up to you. On your path towards healing there too, will be many choices to make.

Some will be easier than others. Some decisions will take weeks to materialize into long-lasting habits. But out of all decisions that you will have to make on your journey towards healing, there is one that you must make if you want to make it to the other side. One that isn't really a choice at all. You must choose yourself. You must choose yourself when you're happy, when you're sad, when you're angry, and when you're disappointed.

You must choose yourself when everyone else tells you that you're not good enough. You must choose yourself when the world forgets about you. When your partner lied, betrayed, and made you feel worthless, you must always choose yourself. When they left you and picked right up with someone else, even then, you must choose yourself. You owe it to yourself to keep walking. To persevere. You're stronger than you think. And if you didn't know that, well, you do now.

For many people, choosing yourself may seem selfish. And I am telling you right now, that's precisely what choosing yourself means. It means putting yourself first. For once, you need to come first. Not your family, not your friends. There is a time and place for everything. And right now, it's time to choose yourself. Your goals matter, your desires do, your pain matters, your hurting matters, your joy matters. I'm not saying you should neglect the people around you. Of course, they matter. Your support system is imperative and deserves to be valued. But not at your own expense. It's okay to say no sometimes. It's okay to want to stay in on a Friday night and do nothing but binge-watch Netflix for 7 hours. It's okay to tell your friends that you need a weekend for yourself. It's okay to not want to talk to anyone for a few days. Listen to your heart. If you need space, give yourself space. If you need help, reach out. If you want to go on a trip, simply book that plane ticket and go. You're your own captain on this journey towards healing. I'm here to guide you, but ultimately, this is your path.

I am not saying be irresponsible and reckless. But do not feel obliged or pressured into doing anything you don't want to do. This is your time, your life, your moment, your healing process. It's time to embrace that journey. And part of that embracing includes choosing yourself. You cannot heal if you're too busy trying to please everyone but yourself. So start putting yourself first.

6.8 - Good Enough

We've come quite far, haven't we? Look at you. I know this hasn't been easy. This journey must feel endless to you. I know it did to me. You've been struggling for so long. I am so incredibly proud of you for fighting through this. I promise you; it'll be worth it. Keep pushing.

If you get nothing but one thing out of this book, get this; **YOU ARE GOOD ENOUGH.** You're worth it. Even if someone tells you otherwise. Even if every person you've met has said to you that you're not good enough, I am telling you that you indeed are good enough. I don't care what they've told you. I don't have to know you to know that you're worth it. I don't need to know what you have done in the past. That's the past. That's behind you. Your past does not define you. You have it in you to change. No matter what you've done, there's a way to come back from it. But that way begins with understanding that you are worthy. Worthy of another chance at love. Just because you've loved the wrong way in the past, doesn't mean you're disqualified from ever loving again. You're not a failure just because you've fallen. You're not worthless just because someone else couldn't see your worth. They may have rejected you, but that's not a reflection of you but rather a reflection of them.

You can be willing and able to give someone the world, but that doesn't mean that they're required to live in it. If someone doesn't want to be part of your life, they do not have to. But that doesn't mean you're worth any less. I know you may be naturally inclined to believe that your self-worth is attached to the people you love. And when they're no longer around, all of a sudden that self-worth quickly departs with them. But you can never let someone else dictate how you value yourself. You simply cannot. It never ends well. I know this is easier said than done. But on your journey towards healing, you must accept this. Otherwise, you cannot move forward. We cannot move forward. Please reread this chapter as much as you need to in order to truly grasp what I am trying to tell you.

For a very long time, I let myself be manipulated into believing that I wasn't good enough. That my past mistakes disqualified me from the right for peace and another chance. I loved someone very deeply, but because of a terrible mistake that I made, I was told by that very person, that I was no longer good enough. I wasn't worthy of her. I took all the mental beatings she gave me without ever second-guessing what was being said. Because I thought I deserved that abuse. I felt I had to take it because, well, I made a mistake, so naturally, I had to pay for it. I became her emotional punchbag for over half a year. Even though we weren't even together for that time, she made it clear that I somehow wasn't worthy of forgiveness, of moving on.

It doesn't matter how much wrong you've done. No one deserves to continuously be told they aren't good enough. If you don't want to be with someone, leave. Let them move on in peace. But don't ever make someone suffer for months, over a mistake that they've clearly learned from and corrected. If you can't forgive the person, then move on.

So if you're like me, plagued with mistakes. Just know that no matter what you've done, you do not deserve to be treated like you aren't worthy. And if someone treats you like that, walk away. And don't you look back. Trust me.

You are worthy. And you certainly are good enough. To heal means to accept your flaws and mistakes. To heal means to understand that despite what may have happened in the past, you are good enough.

On my own road to healing, there were many days where I felt like I wasn't good enough. I felt like I wasn't worth the forgiveness that I so desperately craved. I believed that I wasn't worthy of finding love ever again. That kind of thinking is absolutely detrimental to your healing and overall mental health. You're essentially poisoning yourself with those negative thoughts. The worst thing was that the person I loved the most, the one person who I needed to believe in me, was the person who made me feel that way.

This happens so many times. No matter who caused the breakup or who made a mistake. Don't add another one to the situation by making that person feel like they aren't good enough or that they don't deserve another chance. Maybe they don't deserve another chance with you, but that doesn't mean that they don't deserve another chance with someone else. If you see them trying to turn their life around and better themselves, what gives you the right to manipulate them into believing that they're worthless? Holding someone's mistake over their head is never okay. Let me say that again because you're not hearing me; holding someone else's mistake over their head is NEVER okay. If you can't forgive them, let them go. If you cannot let their mistakes go, you need to let the person go. It is that simple.

And if you're the person who made a mistake, love yourself enough to walk away if the other person cannot move on from what happened. If you're trying to become better and all they're doing is holding you back, then you need to let them go.

You may have hurt the other person, but that doesn't give them the right to hold that mistake over your head for weeks and months to come. Realize your worth, regardless of whether or not you made a mistake. You're good enough even though they walked out of your life and chose someone else. You're good enough even if they did lie to you a hundred times. They betrayed you? You're still good enough. They cheated? You're still good enough. The actions of someone else will never define who you are. The inability of someone else to see your worth doesn't diminish yours. You're unique, you're special, you're pure. They can't take away what they've never given you, to begin with. They didn't make you; they do not define you. You, my friend, are, and always will be good enough.

Part 7 [What Now?]

7.1 - Not a 3-Step Program

Still going strong, are we? I know this journey hasn't been easy. Healing ourselves after suffering a devasting heartbreak and disappointment is one of the hardest things we will ever have to endure. But that is precisely what we are doing. We're enduring. We're prevailing. We will come out of this process stronger and wiser. We've covered a lot so far. And I'm hoping you've taken some of my advice. I've been in your shoes; part of me is still in your shoes. Healing isn't a quick 3-step program that can be accomplished in a week or two. Deep healing from severe mental trauma takes months. You may have to read this book a few times to truly grasp what it takes to become whole again. We've talked about how to heal; one first must admit that they're hurt. I told you that it's okay to not be okay. I mentioned why healing the right way is such an essential aspect of life. I told you from the very beginning that you need to prepare yourself for the next few months because this journey isn't going to be easy. Heartbreak is a war, healing is a war. And we're fighting a battle for our lives every single day. If you want to heal the right way, the only way; then you need to prepare yourself to be uncomfortable for some time. But this is just how it has to be. You may not have chosen this path, but this is where we are. Maybe you didn't cause the destruction, but you're the one who needs to clean it up. This is your responsibility. Not your ex, not your friends, not mine. I can't fix you. I can't make the pain go away. I cannot heal you. Only you can do that. I've merely given you the right tools to win the war that is raging inside of you. So now you're wondering what to do next. You're telling yourself: 'Marvin, I've done everything you've told me to do, but I'm still not where I want to be, now what'?

Now you do what you have to do to keep moving. You persevere despite still deeply grieving the loss of someone you loved. When you've spent years of your life with someone, you can't just expect things to go back to normal after only a few weeks. It's a process. It takes time. It takes so much time. You're in a waiting season, but this waiting season does not have to be a wasted season. You're becoming better. This journey towards healing isn't just about being whole again. It's about being a completely different person. They say pain changes you. And it most certainly does. Pain makes you stronger. And that, my friend, is what you're doing now. You're becoming stronger. You're becoming the person you were always meant to be. You may not see it right now, but little by little, it'll start making sense. Your vision is going to start becoming clearer. Things will soon fall into place. Trust the process. Trust that God has a plan for you.

7.2 - Healing Isn't Linear

One thing that you have to understand about healing is that it isn't linear. Emotional healing isn't like a typical physical wound where you can see the bleeding stop. You can't see the scab forming and falling off. You can't see the scar fading into your skin. No, with emotional trauma, there is no visual confirmation. No validation that it is, in fact, happening. With emotional trauma, there will be days when things get easier. Then there will be days where it'll hurt like hell. And then there will be days, weeks even where you feel like you're not getting anywhere. That's when the 'now what?' feeling starts to overcome you. Some days, the hurt is so far away from you, you'll feel like it didn't happen to you. You'll feel proud of yourself that you brushed the heartbreak so quickly off your shoulders. Some days though, the hurt will be so real that it'll occupy every single fiber in your body. You'll want to scream because of how painful it is. That hurt will consume you on those days.

You know what all those days have in common? They are all days in which you're still healing. The pain doesn't nullify your healing. It doesn't erase your progress. It's just a reminder that healing isn't linear. Healing doesn't abide by some magic formula. On your journey towards healing, there will be times where you'll stumble and fall flat on your face. There will be times when it feels like you're going the wrong way. There will be times when you feel like you can't keep going anymore. But trust me that you're heading in the right direction.

Just because it doesn't look like you're healing, doesn't mean you aren't healing. You can be doing great for weeks at a time, and then there will be that one person who brings up their name and boom, there you are; feeling like you've just been hit by moving truck. You're going to feel discouraged because it's been so long, and all it had to take for you to fall down again was for someone to simply utter that person's name. I am here to tell you that it's okay. Just because you still have bad days, doesn't mean you're not moving forward. It just means that there's still room for more healing. Remember, healing isn't linear. It never has been with anyone else, and it won't be with you.

7.3 - Healing Isn't Pretty

Healing is a beautiful transformation. It's laying to rest the person you once were; broken, shattered, and tainted with disappointment. And creating a new version of yourself. A better one, a stronger one. Healing is putting yourself back together when the world left you broken. Healing is being reborn from the ashes of the old you. It's not turning over the page, it's reinventing a new book. Writing a new story. Your story.

Healing, indeed, is a beautiful thing when you think about it. It's a transformation that takes months of perseverance. Healing from mental trauma is a true testimony to how resilient we humans really are. Yes, healing is a phenomenal process. But it sure isn't pretty. Healing is not just margarita's with the girls on a Friday night, or watching basketball with the guys on Saturday. Healing is not devouring an entire pie of pizza on a lazy Sunday. Healing isn't cutting your hair or dying it brown. It isn't getting a tattoo or landing a new job. Healing isn't signing up for a new gym membership or going on a shopping spree. Healing isn't getting into another relationship. Healing isn't moving out of your parent's house.

All those things can exist while healing. They can all be moments on your path to healing that make the journey a little more comfortable. More tolerable. But that isn't healing. Healing, real genuine healing, is ugly. It's not something you're rushing to post on Instagram. Authentic healing isn't something you're going to tweet about. You know why? Because real healing is when you have random flashbacks of them, and all of a sudden, you're spending the next 20 minutes crying over that person who is no longer part of your life. Real healing is waking up in the morning, and the first thing you notice is how your bed is feeling awkwardly empty without that someone in it. And then crying about it for the next half hour, only to later realize that you're late for work.

Healing is ugly, it's messy, and it isn't something you're going to show off to the world. Because showing real healing off would mean revealing to the world how vulnerable and broken you really are. It would mean to show off all the tears, the puffy red eyes, the breakdowns. Real healing is hearing that person in every song you listen to, it's seeing them at every red light. Real healing is like peeling off your own skin. It's like setting the old you on fire. Real healing is ugly, and it's painful.

Please don't expect this journey to be a nice one. Because it isn't. Don't assume that it'll all be freedom and independence, girls nights, new friendships, getting wine-drunk with your best friend, traveling the world, and making all new happy memories. All that can happen. But I'm afraid that that isn't genuine healing. Real healing is painful. Real healing is setting your old life on fire and letting the light guide you to a new one. A better one.

7.4 - When You're Ready

The other day I was sitting in the all too familiar office of my therapist. I looked at her, and I felt awfully empty. I was bereaved, and my therapist knew it. She asked me how I was doing, and I said 'fine,' although I'm not quite sure why I said that because I didn't convince either of us with that response. I told her how I couldn't believe how some people just move on like that. How do they do it? How do you jump from one relationship to the next? I can't fathom the sheer thought of being with someone else. When will I ever be ready? "You'll know when you're ready," she said in an empathic, almost motherly way. "But will I?" I said quietly. "How do I know when I'm ready to start something new again with someone new?" "You'll simply know, it will feel right," she said.

My therapist was indeed right, you'll know when you're ready to start over again. Dating again after suffering heartbreak is incredibly difficult and scary. I was terrified about opening up to someone months after my relationship had already ended. I knew I didn't have another failed relationship in me. I didn't want to go through another 'talking' stage. I didn't want to learn about someone's favorite color, and their favorite food, and find out what their dreams are. I didn't want to meet someone's parents again. I didn't want to start over with someone. Thinking about opening up to someone again after being so deeply wounded was unimaginable to me back then. I knew that I wasn't ready. I wouldn't be ready for a very long time. But I was okay with that.

In order to step into the life that we deserve to live with the right person, we need to accept that we may have to be alone for some time and wait. Because the right person will come along when you're ready. And that may take a while. Months, even years.

I know that the first thing many people do after heartbreak is to seek the attention of someone else to 'get over' the previous person. In theory, it sounds simple enough, almost like the right thing to do even. But jumping from one sinking ship to the closest shore insight only calls for a disaster waiting to happen. Learn how to swim before attempting to date again. Learn how to be by yourself. Even if it means being alone for a very long time. On your journey towards healing, there will be many times when your friends will urge you to date again. They'll want to set you up with their friend or co-worker. Their intentions are pure, but it's not up to them to decide when you're ready. Only you know when you are, in fact, ready. It can take 8 months, 10 months, a year. There is no right answer. Take all the time in the world. You're ready when you say you're ready.

But just remember; do not project the pain of any past experience on a present opportunity. Don't let yesterday's heartbreak deter you

113

from today's blessing. Not everyone will want to hurt you, I know that may seem hard to believe at this time, but it's the truth. Don't become bitter or cynical just because you've been hurt. The journey towards deep healing is one that avoids those things. There's no room for resentment in your heart if you're on the path to true healing.

I want you to take all the time in the world to heal wholeheartedly. But what I do not wish, is for you to build up these walls around you and block your blessings. I know you're scared; I know you're vulnerable. The wounds are still so raw. But do not mistake other people for your past. They're not your ex. They didn't hurt you. They didn't cut you. People deserve the benefit of the doubt. Don't let your past hurt hinder your ability to take in the good. Those walls you've put up high all around you, yeah, they may protect you. But they also block the light from coming in.

7.5 - Scars Are Beautiful Too

Heartbreak will leave you with trauma, but you know that already. Sometimes that trauma can be minimal; other times, it'll be so severe, it can take a lifetime to overcome. No matter how badly you've been hurt, heartbreak will leave you with scars. Not the kind of scars you can see on your skin when you've cut yourself. No, I'm talking about the type of scars that are deep inside of you. The ones the world can't see, but you can feel. Those scars are more real than anything else you've ever experienced. As time passes, those scars will fade. But they will never truly disappear. You can't undo the damage, but you can heal from it.

We've gotten so far on this journey towards healing. It must have been hell for you at times. I know it was for me. We're almost there, though, the finish line. I can see it on the horizon. But you need to understand one thing before you get there. Heartbreak changes you, and healing changes you. By the time you finish this book and apply all the advice that I've given you, you will indeed be a changed person. You will never be the same. And for that, you should be incredibly proud. Be proud of yourself. For fighting, for surviving.

I want you to be proud of the scars you've been given. I'm a firm believer that there is beauty in the trauma that we've suffered. There's something real about the pain. Of course, it's not pleasant to be left heartbroken, but it's part of life. It's part of being human.

115

I believe that there is beauty in contrast. In the light and the dark days. You can't have one without having the other. I know today might not be the best day of your life, but today is the first day of the rest of your life. Stop looking back. Stop hindering yourself from the endless possibilities that are out there for you. And stop feeling guilty or embarrassed about the trauma you've endured. There's nothing to be ashamed of. Your scars are beautiful too.

Yes, you've loved, and yes, you've been hurt too. You trusted the wrong person, you gave one too many chances, maybe you're the one who hurt someone that you love. And now you're left with the regret of yesterday. Embarrassed and ashamed. But I am here to tell you that there is beauty in those scars. You just can't see it yet. But one day, you will.

I want you to kiss your own scars, love them like you love your favorite TV show. Love them like you love your best friend. Love them, like you love your family. Love your scars, like you loved the person who gave them to you. The path to deep healing is one that embraces what has happened and accepts all that is going to happen. To heal means to fall in love with yourself again, all of you. That includes your scars. Every single last one of them.

I was a very active child. I couldn't stand still for more than 5 minutes without becoming bored out of my mind. One day, when I was a little kid, I played with my older sister in our small apartment back in Germany. Somehow she ended up chasing me and as I was running away from her. I looked back to see where she was when I quickly looked ahead and all of a sudden, I found myself running into the corner of a wall. At full speed. There was so much blood everywhere. My mother had to rush me to the nearest hospital in the back of a taxi. I honestly don't know how I survived that day.

This happened 24 years ago, and 'til this day, I still see the scar on my forehead every single morning when I look into the mirror. I can touch the scar, and I won't feel a thing. I can feel the scar tissue differentiating from my healthy skin. I'm not ashamed of my scar or embarrassed by it. Because that scar is a constant reminder of how 24 years ago, I suffered an injury that had the potential to end my life. But it didn't. I survived. I overcame that injury. Why would I be ashamed of surviving such a devastating trauma? I embrace my scars. They are proof that I overcame destruction. Emotional scarring is no different than a physical one. Don't be ashamed that you've been struggling with grief. Don't hide the fact that it took you months to overcome your breakup. Be proud of it. You survived an emotional trauma that could have destroyed you. But it didn't. I don't know of a more beautiful struggle. There is beauty in chaos, beauty in destruction. Remember, you have not lived until you have died. It is clear, my friend, that your scars are beautiful too. Never forget that.

7.6 - Through Broken Pieces, We Mend

No matter how broken you are, how horrible your breakup has been, or how much you've lost; you're not a lost cause. Yes, you may be broken, but you know what? So has everyone else at one point. Things break, people betray us, they lie to our face, rob us of our peace. Humans are flawed, and it's only normal that there will be times when things end up breaking. The breaking isn't necessarily the biggest problem. It's fixing the brokenness after the fact, this is what is so important. Overcoming your struggles is what really matters. No one wakes up in the morning and says, "Hey, I wish I was broken." No one does. But being human includes broken pieces. We break, it happens.

And through those broken pieces, we mend. We find out what we are truly made of. During our darkest moments, our broken moments, we find out how to persevere. We build a character, stronger and more resilient than we could have ever imagined. When we break, we die a little just to be reborn again as greater version.

You are real, and being real means you break. Maybe not always into a million pieces, but in dozens and sometimes hundreds of pieces. And just as you break, so can you mend. For when you die, you can be reborn again.

There is a tradition in Japan called Kintsugi. This is when a piece of ceramic breaks or cracks, and instead of throwing the whole thing away or gluing it back together to pretend it didn't break, the repair technique is to cover those cracks and breaks by repairing them with a precious metal like gold, silver or platinum. This is meant to demonstrate how brokenness can be incredibly valuable.

There is a beauty in the broken, and the Japanese see the joining of the pieces back together as part of the ceramic's history, part of its journey. Not something to cover up and hide or be embarrassed about. In a society that throws broken things away, what a beautiful idea to see something for what it is and find the beauty in all of it. To mend the broken pieces with something even more aesthetically pleasing and valuable than the ceramic piece it started out as.

Just like the unfortunate moments that put us on this heartbreaking path and the broken parts that we feel we are made of; we need to embrace them all because they hold a certain type of beauty. The brokenness makes us better; it makes us even more valuable, not less. This is the beauty of imperfection.

I know you didn't plan to be on this journey. In a perfect world, you would have never been heartbroken, you would have never been hurt. But we do not live in a perfect world. So find the beauty in your brokenness. And instead of covering it up, instead of pretending they didn't hurt you, embrace your brokenness, embrace your hurt, embrace the process.

When we break and join back together, we become stronger. We finally see ourselves for what we are in all of our vulnerability. Even when we feel broken. And it is through those broken pieces that we mend. And we become more and more beautiful each time.

Part 8: [How's Life on The Other Side?]

8.1 - What Moving On Is Really Like

Healing from heartbreak and disappointment is a long process. It involves acknowledging the hurt, acknowledging what went wrong, it's accepting what happened, that you've been affected dearly by someone's absence. It's recognizing that they've left a mark on you. Healing is to take responsibility for things that may have been out of your control. Healing is to forgive. It's to reinvent yourself and find out who you really are. To heal is to love. The flaws, the imperfections, the wounds, the scars. To heal means to be reborn again out of your own ashes, as a better, new, improved version of yourself. This is what healing is. We've been on this road to healing for a while now. You know what it takes to heal. You know what you have to let go of, and you know what you have to hold on to.

But if we genuinely want to heal, we must also learn how to move on. And many don't know what moving on is really like. Because healing and moving on are not the same. Just because you've moved on, doesn't mean you've healed.

Moving on isn't like an anniversary or a birthday, you can't count down its arrival. You can't mark it on a calendar or announce it to your 2,000 Instagram followers. Moving on isn't something you plan for. You won't be able to call your friends to celebrate with you when it happens. Moving on isn't even a singular event. It isn't merely hitting a light switch. No one moves on in an instant because although deep down we know we have to; our mind will play tricks and prevent us from moving on (at first).

You move on once. And then you move on again. And then again and again and again. You'll move on from your ex the first time you forget what kind of car they are driving. It happens suddenly and unexpectedly. You'll move on when you wake up in the morning, and the first thing that comes to your mind isn't them. You're moving on when you find yourself going 4,5,6,7 hours without thinking about them. Every hour that you spent without them on your mind is a victory to you. You move on when you go to the grocery store, and you don't automatically have that nostalgic feeling of when the two of you would walk down the aisle and pick out your favorite ice cream. You move on when you go out for drinks with your friends, and your first instinct won't be to text them at 2AM. You move on the first time you get exciting news, and it doesn't occur to you to call them. You move on when you're finally winning in life again, and your instinct isn't to share it with that person. When you fail in life, and you won't feel the need to lean on them for support.

You move on when you've reached a point in your healing process when your life finally belongs to you again. Your triumphs, your failures, they become yours once again. To celebrate, to endure. You move on when you've found yourself comfortable in your current situation. Not complacent in life, just satisfied with living life without them. You're moving on when you miss them, but you don't want them back. You're moving on when you've accepted the fact that they're not coming back, that there will be no redo. And as sad as that may be, it will be okay.

You will move on from that person a thousand times, a thousand different ways. And there is nothing wrong or abnormal about that. You're human. Moving on isn't a simple nor easy decision. It takes time, patience, and understanding.

So what is moving on really like? Well, moving on looks a lot like this:

One day you forget the taste. The next, you forget the smell. Then the touch. Then the laugh. Then the smile. Then the jokes. Then the eyes, the hair, the hands, the feet. You forget the socks. You forget the fingers, the toes, the sex. You forget what their heartbeat sounded like. You forget how their eyes looked at 7 in the morning when the sunlight would just hit them right. You forget how you felt like they belonged to you. You forget the words; finally, you forget their voice. You forget how their lips tasted on yours. You forget how your hands felt locked inside theirs.

You want to know what moving on is like? Moving on is not like beginning a new chapter, it's like starting a new book — with each turned page, the last story you read fades into the background. Day by day, they fade away. A fairy tale that becomes just another book on a shelf. Every day that passes is another day that makes forgetting them easier. Page by page, memory by memory; their presence in your life becomes nothing but a distant memory. One you'll barely remember at times. Moving on is when you begin to forget the intricacies of a character you knew intimately; you forget what her favorite color was. You forget his best friend's name. What she does for a living. You forget what sport he played in high school. You forget who they were and what made them unique. This will be equally as beautiful as it will be heartbreaking. There was a time when they meant everything to you. A time when you couldn't imagine living without them. But those times are long gone. And moving on is being okay with that.

Moving on means being at peace with the idea that you will never see that person again. It's accepting that your lips won't touch theirs ever again. They will never lay in your arms again. No more breakfast, lunch, or dinners. No more movie dates and lazy Sundays. No more vacations together. Moving on is accepting that there will be no more "one more." Moving on is putting to rest the dreams and hopes you had with that person. The perfect wedding you two pictured in your head. That big house in Texas you two planned for. The honeymoon in Bora Bora that you guys couldn't stop raving about. The ring you wanted to buy her. You know, the one with the rose gold band and 9mm round moissanite stone. The one she told you about a hundred times. And each time her eyes would light up like it was all she ever wanted, and in turn, so did yours, because the truth is; seeing her happy was all you ever wanted. Moving on is coming to terms with the fact that that person's part in your life has come to an abrupt end. And that there is nothing you or anyone else can do about it. Moving on is beginning to understand that not everyone we love is meant to stay. And perhaps that will be the hardest lesson we will have to come to terms with on this road to healing.

You two were exciting, and the possibilities you had together seemed endless. Moving on is knowing that they still are endless. For you, for them, but not for two of you. Somewhere between then and now, here and there, something happened. Something broke between the two. Something that neither of you could fix. You can always fix yourself, but unfortunately, you can't always fix a relationship. Moving on means to let the broken pieces go, before cutting yourself any more than you already have. Moving on is freedom. Moving on is a new start.

8.2 - The Blessing Might Look like a Wound

I know that this part right here may be confusing to you at first. Or even for a very long time. It certainly took me a long time to accept that my wounds were, in fact, blessings after all. You might wonder how what you're currently going through could even remotely be considered a blessing. This is because right now, you're not thinking logically. You're emotional, vulnerable, and hurt. All of which is absolutely normal, and it's okay to feel that way. We all do at one point or another on our road to healing from a devastating heartbreak. But what you are failing to understand is that you are too close to the destruction to see the true beauty behind it. The blessing. All you see right now is loss and pain. Because you're standing in it. You're surrounded by it, you're drowning in it. But you'll soon realize once you're out of that mess, things aren't always what they seem to be. Right now, you're staring into an abyss of grief and disappointment. But rest assured that you will overcome this. You will persevere. And one day you will look back at this experience, this loss, and you'll be thankful for it. You may even be glad it happened. And that is the ultimate testimony to healing. Accepting what was, embracing what is, and celebrating what will come. Because what lies ahead is so much greater than what you've left behind. Or what left you behind.

See, the thing with blessings is that everyone thinks blessings are the great news we get told. The new job, the raise, the engagement, the graduation, the birth of a new child. People connect blessings to new beginnings, to improved circumstances. And yes, those are all blessings. But those aren't the only blessings there are. Us humans love having things our way right when we want it. We're obsessed with instant gratification, and when things don't go our way when we want it, we don't think it could be considered a blessing. This isn't the case at all. Blessings aren't always instant. They aren't always immediately visible. And they aren't always wrapped in new beginnings.

The blessings that make the most significant impact in our lives are the ones we would kindly decline if we were given a choice because we don't know any better. But that's precisely why we don't have a say in those blessings. The most significant blessings we experience are the ones that are wrapped in painful endings and agonizing disappointment. The blessings that come with tears and sleepless nights. The ones that come with rejection and betrayal. The blessings that come with breakups. Those are the true blessings in disguise. The ones that we only recognize after we heal. After we let go of the emotional baggage. Those are the hardest blessings to understand, but they're the most important ones. The ones that we don't usually know how to accept, but we know that we're being protected from something unfavorable and guided toward something better. It is easy to accept a job promotion as a blessing. But you know what is really hard? Accepting that losing the person you wanted to spend the rest of your life with is a blessing too. Because endings my dear friend, are blessings also, as they are the doorway to new beginnings. And one day, you will agree with me and not shake your head in disbelieve. That, I promise you. Know that one day, you will look back and see that breakup, not as the end, but as the starting point. As the pivot that turned everything around. As the thing that gave you the courage to try something new, something that would come to beautiful fruition. Let yourself realize that every wonderful thing that you've experienced is so because something else ended, not in spite of it. Sometimes things must end for there the be room for something new, something better. And yes, there are times when the things that have to end are tremendous and magical and special. But that doesn't mean that you're supposed to stop there. It doesn't mean that there isn't something else waiting behind that door.

One day you, too, will realize that a blessing will often look like a wound at first. But soon enough, you'll see that that wound will be the greatest thing that ever happened to you.

8.3 - Behind Your Breakup, Lies Your Breakthrough

Ironically enough, both of my most significant breakthroughs in life happened right after two severe breakups. The first one caused me to fall in love with traveling. I found comfort in my own solitude. The breakup was the reason why I created my own website; 'Embrace The Layover' and started blogging. That's when I began nurturing my writing skills. That breakup was excruciating, and it threw me into a 4-month long depression. Climbing out of that abyss was the hardest thing I ever had to do. But I made it. I survived. And I am better for it.

Fast forward a few years, and yet again, I found myself at the end of another relationship. My second one. This time things weren't quite as simple. I was stuck for half a year in a terrible, toxic situation that robbed me of my joy, peace, and self-worth. The absolute worst 6 months of my life. A time that I will never get back. But I learned so many valuable lessons through that time. Through that breakup, I found Jesus. I discovered my real purpose and what I wanted to do with my life. I finally knew that writing was a crucial component of living in my purpose. That breakup is the reason I wrote this book. That breakup is the reason I get to help so many other people who are struggling with the same demons I've struggled with. That breakup forced me on a path that I wouldn't have chosen if given a choice. But I now know that I needed to be on that path. The path to healing. The path to self-improvement. The way that led me to you.

That breakup was my breakthrough. Without it, I wouldn't be who I am. And who I am is someone I am mighty proud of. Just know that your breakup can be your most significant breakthrough. But you have to put in the work. It's either sink or swim. And I need you to get swimming.

8.4 - Time For a Revelation

Look how far you've come. You're still here. I'm still here. I told you at the beginning of this journey that I would be here 'til the end.

I'm proud of you. I know it hasn't been easy. But you're almost there. You've almost made it through this devastating storm. We're at the part of this journey towards healing, where it is time to reflect. Reflect on these past weeks and months. What we've been through. How far we've come. I know that you didn't plan for this to happen. I know you never thought you'd need to read a book about healing because you didn't expect to be left broken. Your life wasn't supposed to be the way it is now. And when you look back at what happened to you, you may be inclined to feel resentment. There once was a person in your life that meant an incredible amount to you. They were supposed to support you. And love you. And be there for you. But when you're looking around, there's no one there. You're all alone. They lied, they walked away, betrayed you, used you. They choose someone else over you. And that is why you may feel that resentment towards that person.

On the other hand, when you reflect on the past, you may also come across regret. Regret because you made mistakes that resulted in the end of your relationship. Regret because you've lied, you've betrayed someone's trust. You were in the wrong. Both of these feelings have no room on our road to healing. Now, they are both really one and the same. Regret is just resentment turned inward. Regret is resenting yourself instead of resenting someone else. Neither of those feelings will be of any use if you want to heal. Maybe you're the reason the relationship ended. Perhaps you lied. You made a mistake or 5. So when it's time to reflect, you'll be inclined to feel just that; regret.

There is a type of reflection that leads to regret, and there's a type of reflection that will lead to resentment. But the right kind of reflection, the one that we absolutely need to complete our healing, is the kind that leads to resolution. Before you finish with this book, I want you to set the record straight about what really happened in your situation. I don't want you to feel guilty for what you may have done that caused these terrible events to unfold. I don't want you to feel resentment towards that person for breaking you. I want you to set the record straight and acknowledge that you're glad that it happened. That heartbreak, that breakup, that disappointment. I want you to be glad that it happened. You may not have planned to be here, but you are here. And this is precisely where you're supposed to be. You do not have to let your outlook on life be defined by the events that brought you to this point.

Everything you went through made you better. There is not a single thing in your life that has happened that wasn't supposed to happen. God has positioned you to be exactly where you are right now. Before we continue on our road towards healing, I need you to first make a revision.

And what I mean by that is that I need you to look back on what has happened to you, and I need you to change your outlook on those events. If you genuinely want to heal, then I need you to revise your view on what really happened to you.

I've noticed for quite some time now, that when I write, the magic doesn't happen when I write the first draft. Or the second draft. Or even the third draft. Not at all. But it is in the revision where the true potential of my writing gets revealed. When I go over something over and over again, I'll start to see the true purpose of it. I begin to see the true potential. But this revelation doesn't happen overnight. It takes time. The same concept applies to healing as well. What I am trying to tell you is that maybe there are things that happened to you where you are getting the story wrong. And I need you to see it differently. Yes, they left you for someone else, but where you see a devastating loss, I see a tremendous blessing through protection. Because if they left you for someone else when things got hard, they'd leave them when things get hard too. You dodged a bullet. Yeah, it sucks, and that bullet may have wounded you, but it didn't kill you. It's better to walk away from the situation limping, then to get crippled with a terrible burden. The burden of loving the wrong person, the right way, for far too long. It's better to lose two years than to lose twenty. Because sometimes the fire inside of you has to die, for there to be room for a new flame to be born. And a new fire inside of you will rise again. That I promise you.

8.5 - I'm Glad it Happened

Resolution is not an event; it is a decision. It is the decision to not only accept what has happened to you but, more importantly, to be glad that it happened to you. There are some things that you went through that you didn't like. There are things that you went through that hurt. And not just a little bit. No, I mean those things hurt you so severely, death seemed enticing at one point. Trust me, I know. Some things happened to you that you wouldn't have chosen if you had the opportunity. Things happened to you that you wouldn't wish upon your worst enemy. But they happened. And now that you've been through this terrible experience, there is something that you've learned from it. You've learned through what you've been through. And it made you who you are today. It made you better. And for that, you need to be glad that it happened. You may have carried some incredible burdens with you. You've been chained to your misfortune. But can I let you in on a little secret? You're freer than everyone else, you know. What happened to you was terrible. You didn't like it, didn't enjoy it. It didn't make sense while you were right in the middle of it. But you'll soon realize (if you haven't already) that what you've been through has only made you stronger. Has only made you better.

Here is a revision that I'll need you to make; stop calling yourself the victim of your current circumstance. You cannot heal until you've stopped pitying yourself over what others have done to you. You're not a hostage to your past. You're not a hostage to what went wrong. You're not a hostage to the endless lies that they've told you. You cannot be a victim AND a victor. You have to choose one. And as your journey to healing is slowly coming to an end, I'm going to need you to make the right choice. I want you to revise some of the stuff in your story and understand what really happened. What happened to you wasn't what you've expected, but it turned you into a new person, a better person.

Revision is the final piece of the puzzle on the journey towards healing. Because if you don't change your outlook on what happened to you, you'll never be able to truly heal. I'll need you to look back on this journey, on what happened to you. And I'll need you to rewrite the story, the real story. Revise it. Because if you don't, you'll continue to carry around the mentality that you're trapped in the situation, stuck with what they've done to you, trapped with how they value you. And you cannot continue to move forward like that. Because you haven't truly let go yet. Not really. You cannot let go of them, until you've let go of what they've done to you, of what you've done to them, of what you've done to each other.

If you want to heal, truly and genuinely heal, then you must relinquish all that is holding you back. All that has kept you chained to your misfortune. You don't have to like what it felt like to appreciate the change that it has created.

When I look at my own personal story, I still find myself in disbelief at times. It took a long time for me to understand what happened. Part of me never really figured it all out, but I've made peace with that. I've made my own closure.

I honestly wouldn't have chosen what I went through, but I wouldn't change it either. I am glad that it happened. And mind you, what happened to me, I wouldn't wish on anyone. I've struggled with an immense loss. There was a woman that I deeply loved. She was my life, my heart, my world. I would have done anything for her. But I've hurt her, and she didn't deserve that. But what she put me through for half a year, almost destroyed me. How one person can do that to another, I still don't understand, and I don't think I ever will.

But despite all of that, something good came out of her departure. She helped me find God and fueled my passion for writing. But not by staying in my life, but rather by leaving. The greatest gift she ever gave me was leaving me. I didn't want to lose the person that I once so desperately loved. I didn't want to say goodbye to our future. But what I failed to realize at the time was that the woman I loved died a long time ago. The person I once knew, the person I wanted to have children with, had died many months before. She wasn't the same person I fell in love with. So her walking out of my life was the best thing she ever did for me. And today, I can say without a doubt that I am glad that it happened.

And I want you to look at your current situation and feel the same way towards it. I want you to be glad that it happened. Whatever that it may be for you. I want you to look at this heartbreak as an opportunity for growth, rather than yet another failed relationship. I want you to be glad that it happened. The thing that other people feel sorry for you about. Be glad for your weakness, as it led you to a more profound strength. Don't let them feel sorry for you. Be glad that it happened. Be glad about it. Not the pain, I'm not telling you to be glad about that, but be glad that within the pain there is a purpose. Yes, you cried about it, endless nights. You wished it went away. You wished the pain would just stop already. When would it be enough? I know every minute laying in that pain felt like an eternity. But now you're standing over those ruins, newborn. Better than ever before. Be glad about it.

I'm glad that they've rejected me. It showed me that God was enough, and I don't need them.

I want you to look at your situation in the same way. Aren't you glad that the storm stripped away everything that you didn't need? Everything that wasn't supposed to stay. Aren't you glad that you're not spending another day carrying any more dead weight? No more toxic behavior. No more fighting. No more lying. No more stressing out over a situation that was never sustainable. No more worthless relationships. Aren't you glad? Aren't you glad that God has closed that door? So that you wouldn't spend years of your life in the wrong room. Be glad that it happened. You're finally free. You might not be able to smile when you're saying it, but you're getting there. And that is what healing really is. It's knowing that you're not fully okay just yet, but one day not too far away, you will be. So I'm glad it happened. I'm glad for the battles. I'm glad for the tears, the sleepless nights, the disappointments, the betrayal.

8.6 – Time to Part Ways

So this is it, my friend, this is the end of our road to healing; together. I must admit something to you. I don't know your specific circumstance. I don't know what happened to you that caused your heartbreak. But the brutal truth is; merely reading this book once won't make all your problems go away. It's not a magic wand that erases all the pain. I am not going to lie to you and pretend otherwise. I don't expect you to close this book and be completely healed. I wish it were that simple. But you and I both know, that when it comes to love, loss, and heartbreak, things are never simple.

Healing is an art. An art that we must master if we want to live a truly fulfilling life. If we're going to create healthy, long-lasting relationships, we must learn how to heal entirely and correctly. And this is no one's responsibility but your own. Your next relationship won't fix you. And it isn't someone else's job to break down the walls that you've put up. It isn't their job to mend your broken heart. That's your job. And you need to do it before getting into another relationship.

I told you we'd walk this journey together. I stayed with you until the end. I'm still here. But we've reached the end of our journey together. This is where we must part ways. Not because I don't want to continue to guide you, but it's your time to be your own compass. I've navigated you through these traitorous waters. But the worst is behind you. Now you must find your own way back home. And no one can tell you where home is for you. Because my home isn't your home, and your home isn't mine. Home isn't a place you can type into your GPS. It's not an actual location. Home is where you can be, well, you. And that perhaps will be the hardest battle you'll ever face; finding your way home. But on this road to healing, we've fought many battles. And you've overcome them all. You're stronger than you could possibly imagine. So this battle, you too, will win.

You will have good days, and you will have bad ones. But do not let the bad days overshadow all the progress you've made. Remember, healing isn't linear. And just because you've healed, doesn't mean you won't still miss them at some point. When you truly love someone, I mean really love them; part of you will always love them. They're part of you, part of your story. And there's nothing that you or anyone can do to change that. There's nothing wrong with that either. All it means is that at one point in time, this person was your person. The person you wanted to do life with, the person you wanted to grow old and have kids with. At one point in time, that person was someone who you let live inside of you. And to be honest, you can't erase the home that they've made inside your heart. And you don't have to. Healing isn't about pretending that the two of you never happened. It's admitting that you two at one point had something special, something magical. Until the day that magic tragically got lost.

8.7 - I Will Be Your Lighthouse

Throughout this journey, I've guided you, encouraged you, supported you. But it's time you start being on your own now. You have it in you to be your own compass, to be your own rock, your own lifeline. But if for whatever reason you lose your way again, I will be there for you to guide you home. I will be your lighthouse in the dark. I will leave the light on, and I'll guide you to safety if you lose hope. I've been in your shoes. I know that trouble is coursing through your veins. I understand that this journey has cost you so much. I know you gave it your all just to make it through.

If you look into the distance, you'll see me there. I'll be your lighthouse. I will leave the light on. I will guide you home. I will be here if you need me.

Part 9: [My Final Gift to You]

To C.

You were my greatest blessing and most profound disappointment. The best and worst thing that has ever happened to me. I honestly can't believe it took me this long to realize how unsustainable our relationship really was. We were never genuinely compatible, and that was the problem. I just wish we didn't tear each other apart only to realize that we weren't meant for each other. What we did to each other, neither one of us deserved. You deserved better from me, and I deserved so much better from you. We both didn't deserve this. I know you never truly loved me; instead, you just loved being with someone, and that someone just happened to be me at the time. After all this time, I finally understand what we were, and what we simply weren't. This was never meant to be. And I realize that now.

There are no words to adequately explain how much you've hurt me by doing what you did. It was so incredibly vindictive and selfish of you. My heart is still aching at the sheer thought of it. We could have walked away from this, intact and whole, a long time ago. But you had to make it your mission to destroy me in your quest to move on. Part of me thinks that you enjoyed doing this to me. Was it payback for all the awful things that I did to you? If so, you sure have a way of getting back at people. You made your point. I hope you're happy. I hope it was worth it.

After all this time, and after all that I gave to you, it is time to finally put this chapter of my life to rest. This is me doing the one thing that I could never do, the one thing you are so profoundly good at; this is my parting, my final gift to you. This is me letting you go.

Thank you for giving up on me. For walking away when I so desperately wanted you to stay. You set me free. And perhaps, that was the most significant thing you have ever done for me.

I remember that one night in Sydney like it was yesterday. We were fighting, like so many other nights. I didn't want to lose you. I wasn't ready to part ways. I was so weak. But I now know, that our relationship should have ended right then and there. There I was, lying on top of you. My head on your chest, tears streaming down my face, asking you not to leave. But deep down, I knew it was time, but I couldn't bring myself to let go. Your heartbeat was pumping so intensely. I can still feel it pulsing through my veins, even though it's now 19 months later. It still haunts me 'til this day.

But I am so much stronger now. I know that this is the right decision, despite it being the hardest thing that I've ever had to do. This is long overdue. It's time for me to let go of the pieces of us that I couldn't let go of before. You were my home for such a long time, but it's time to move out. To move on. And I've finally conceptualized this.

I hope that one day, you get to experience true love for someone else, like the way I loved you. I can't explain what that feels like, you'll just know. I pray you'll find that kind of love. Because that kind of love is magic. That's what you were to me once; magic.

Goodbye, once and for all.

Printed in Great Britain
by Amazon

57030903R00098